I Should
Have Gone Home

I Should Have Gone Home

Tripping Up Around the World

Edited by
Roger Rapoport
Bob Drews
& Kim Klescewski

RDR Books
Berkeley, California

I Should Have Gone Home

RDR Books
2415 Woolsey Street
Berkeley, CA 94705
Phone: (510) 595-0595
Fax: (510) 228-0300
E-mail: read@rdrbooks.com
Website: www.rdrbooks.com

ISBN: 1-57143-107-1

Library of Congress Catalog Card Number 2004195529

Editors: Roger Rapoport, Bob Drews and Kim Klescewski
Cover Photograph: Daryl Chapman
Design and Production: Richard Harris
Proofreading: Dianne Yeakey

"Annie Get Your Stun Gun" by Ellen Creager is reprinted
by permission of the *Detroit Free Press*

Distributed in Canada by Starbooks Distribution,
100 Armstrong Way, Georgetown, ON L7G 5S4

Distributed in the United Kingdom and Europe by
Roundhouse Publishing Ltd., Millstone, Limers Lane,
Northam, North Devon EX39 2RG, United Kingdom

Printed in Canada

Dedicated to the memory of

Leroy Aarons

author, editor, teacher and friend

Table of Contents

Preface:

Life, Liberty and the Pursuit of Unhappiness

by Roger Rapoport

RDR BOOKS, A NEW CALIFORNIA PUBLISHER, released a book in 1994 based on the premise that travelers and non-travelers alike would be fascinated by disaster stories. Although this book, *I Should Have Stayed Home,* included the works of prominent authors such as Paul Theroux and Barbara Kingsolver, as well as distinguished travel writers like Jan Morris, Pico Iyer and Tony Wheeler, many other contributors were making their first appearances in print. In the wrong place at the right time, they offered stories that brought a smile to readers who'd been there and hopefully not done that.

A decade later you are holding the fifth volume in this humor series that has set an international standard in hopelessness. These travel humor books, translated into more than a dozen languages, have transcended geography, language and class, not to mention national origin. From the religious pilgrim to the elitist determined to recreate the Orient Express luxury experience, we all enjoy hearing about someone else who has seen a good trip go horribly wrong.

Before starting the *I Should Have Stayed Home* series, I had spent many years working as a travel writer, telling newspaper and magazine readers where to go. For those who were eager to have me along for the ride, I even wrote guidebooks, often in tandem with experts who were seasoned editors and travel agents. Imagine my surprise when I learned that the audience for stories about bad trips was significantly broader than the audience for our Getaway guides to England, Colorado, the Southwest and California.

You may wonder what is wrong with travelers. Is no mountain high enough or river wide enough for them? Why don't they turn around when a blizzard sets in or they see the obvious peril of a Class 5 rapids? Why do they take all these chances when they don't have to? Wouldn't it make more sense for them to spend their money on a package tour to EuroDisney, where the wine flows freely, luggage is never lost and the bathrooms are checked for cleanliness every 15 minutes? The answer, my friends, is not blowing in the wind. Rather, it is in these pages, and I welcome you to join me to meet some of the winners of our international travel disaster contests held in association with bookstores, libraries and newspapers from Portland to London's Putney neighborhood.

One of my favorite disaster stories involves yours truly when my rental car was stolen outside a bookstore in Denton, Texas. Naturally, I was giving a talk on the *I Should Have Stayed Home* series. The police never found the Dodge, my clothes, laptop, books or a box of bright red *I Should Have Stayed Home* buttons. Six weeks later I received a long, handwritten letter from a woman in South Carolina who had read about my incident. She had seen my belongings for sale at a flea market. Unfortunately, my correspondent explained, no one appeared to be buying the hot RDR books.

That, of course, must be an aberration. For the books, and the stories, multiply.

In fact, traffic in these tales of humor and horror is so brisk that RDR Books can no longer accommodate all the wonderful material sent to us. Indeed, our inbox is so full that we are now planning new single-topic books on subjects like hotels and food. Yes, in the time it takes you to read this sentence another world traveler will be on their way down the River of No Return having paid for the privilege.

Talk show hosts and journalists frequently ask the RDR editorial team, Bob Drews, Kim Klescewski and myself, to name our favorite *I Should Have Stayed Home* stories. This question is a little like asking a parent to single out his or her favorite child. With these pieces frequently reprinted in newspapers, magazines and anthologies, it's hard to pick out a grand prize winner. Suffice it to say we find something endearing in every story we read.

But there certainly are moments along the way that enjoy a permanent home in our collective memory bank. Who could ever forget the moment in *I Should Have Gone Home* when Dian Fossey urges our writer Kelly Stewart to stalk Rwandan Gorilla poachers with a Beretta smuggled into the country deep inside an English Christmas cake? Or what about the scene in *I Really Should Have Stayed Home* when a lawyer tells Brian Abrahams that his parking fine for blocking a line of Brussels trams added up to $85,000?

Tales of troubled travel like these resonate with our fans from Madagascar to Mongolia. Certainly, we hope none of this ever happens to you. But if it does, we would love to hear all about it.

No Crime and Lots of Punishment

by Karin Palmquist

"DON'T YOU HAVE ANYTHING A BIT MORE . . . INCONSPICUOUS?"
my friend Elena asked the Avis car rental agent as we
walked around the electric-blue Seat Cordoba at the office
in downtown Tallinn, Estonia. "Like a rust-covered Lada
for example?"

The car glimmered in the winter sun. We were in Estonia with four days to spare. We wanted to see St. Petersburg. Why not take a little road trip?

Avis was the only rental company that allowed customers to drive its cars over the border into Russia. And this
dayglo Seat was all they had available.

We threw in our bags and headed for the highway feeling like a moving target.

At the Estonian border town of Narva, we had to pay a
brand new border crossing tax. That took place at a booth
inside a gated industrial area across town. But first we had
to pick up the ticket necessary to pay the tax. Of course
the ticket vendors couldn't take our money. That was the
responsibility of two people in another booth, and they
couldn't issue the tax receipt. That was the duty of a pair
of workers at a third window. And the two people who issue the receipt can't open the gate to let you out. I couldn't
understand why Narva's unemployment rate was 18 percent.

Next came an inspection of us, our papers and our car. Vacation in Russia in February? Now, what were we really going to do there? After an hour of interrogation in 5-degree weather, they went on to inspect the car. The lock to the car trunk had frozen solid in the cold. Slowly they started to take the car apart, cushion by cushion, eager to access the trunk from the back seat.

After finding frozen stiff clothing and no written materials more suspicious than my Swedish-language edition of *Crime and Punishment,* they let us go.

We made it only about a mile before we saw the blue lights on a police cruiser. An officer signaled for us to pull over.

"What's the problem?" we asked.

"Speeding."

We were well aware of the speed limit and were sure we hadn't been speeding, since we didn't know the way and the road was streaked with patches of ice.

"Officer," we tried.

"Speeding!"

"How much?" we sighed.

"One hundred dollars."

We haggled the fine down to $10, paid in dollars.

Just down the road we were stopped again.

"Speeding," an officer in a gray overcoat said. "Straff." Straff, we had learned, meant fine.

"No speeding. No straff."

"Da. Straff."

"Njet. No straff."

The officer shrugged his shoulders. Ok, then, no straff. He let us go. We couldn't believe it. We tried the same thing the next time we were pulled over.

"Oh, yes. Straff," insisted a short officer with a neck like a bear's as he pointed to his gun.

"But of course. Straff."

The old, tattered Swedish edition of *Crime and Punishment* in the backseat was called *Brott och Straff*. It seemed rather fitting, driving to the beat of Dostoyevsky's famous novel as beat cops tracked us down.

We continued all the way to St. Petersburg. Start, stop, start, stop. Sometimes we paid, sometimes we didn't.

Hours later we reached our destination. We found the old Intourist hotel on the Vyborg side of St. Petersburg. We had pre-booked and my friend Elena went to check in while I argued with the parking lot attendant.

"Twenty dollars."

"But the price on the sign says $10."

"Twenty dollars."

"But it says 10. I only need one space."

"Nice car, you can pay more."

That was it. We weren't driving anymore until we had to leave. We walked out to hail a cab. Lots of cars stopped, but no cab. When the thermometer reads below zero, there is no point in worrying about the cold. For three days we let strangers guide us around St. Petersburg: to the Hermitage, the Church of the Resurrection and what must be St. Petersburg's only rodeo club.

At the end of our stay I tried to pack the musical mirror that had woken us up each morning at 7:30 p.m. to the strains of Swan Lake. But it wouldn't fit in my suitcase.

After stuffing our pockets with $5 notes, we braced ourselves for the return journey. Our departure down fabled Nevsky Prospekt was slowed by heavy traffic and three police stops.

"I saw you," the first officer said. "Flying down the street."

"But we came from over there," we said, pointing the other way.

"Oh. No left turn," said the officer with the look of a politician who had lost the popular vote and been named President of the United States by the Supreme Court.

Outside of town our delays continued as a fourth officer pulled us over. "Speeding," he explained.

A little bit later, we were detained for, surprise, the same reason. By now the traffic fines exceeded the cost of our petrol.

"We weren't speeding," insisted Elena.

The officer waved for her to follow him to a roadside shack. When I tried to accompany her, another officer pointed his gun my way and suggested I stay in the car.

Alone in the shack with three officers, Elena attempted to negotiate. By the time she walked out, the last of our hard currency was gone.

Just before reaching the Estonian border we were hauled in to another roadside shack. We had no dollars left. When we tried to pay with local currency, the officers confiscated our driver's licenses. By now we were screaming and crying. The officers finally relented, in exchange for all our remaining funds. As soon as our licenses were returned we decided to forget about the speed limit and make a dash for the border. Although we really were speeding, no one pulled us over.

"Welcome to Estonia," said the border guards. We kissed them both. Neither of them seemed surprised.

Rock On

by Polly Greist

YEE-HAA! OUR FOUR-FAMILY GROUP FROM OREGON had won a permit in the lottery that controls access to the great wilderness rivers of Idaho—the Selway, Snake and, in our case, the Salmon. Months of organization, strategizing potlucks and to-do lists flew by, the only blip was a worrisome letter from the forest service that the shuttle road to put-in had been washed out by the sudden spring thaw when virtually the entire snowpack had come down in one sizzling week and the Salmon roared into full flood.

"No worries!" promised John our shuttle driver and local contact in Idaho, pointing out that our launch date was yet two months away, plenty of time for road repairs. And indeed, the deluge receded, the road emerged from the mud and river running on the Salmon settled into its natural summertime routine. At least until the day we arrived.

On that sultry, smoky afternoon we pulled our gear-laden trucks and trailers into the little town of Salmon, jumping off point for all voyagers seeking the "River of No Return." A young firefighter from town had died the night before in a lightning-sparked blaze that was today raging out of control in the watershed adjacent to our put-in. Our washed-out, rebuilt shuttle road had just been shut down to all traffic.

"No worries!" proclaimed John, predicting that the

road would open again the next day. If it didn't, all our months of planning would be for naught since our permit (strictly enforced) allowed us to launch on July 25 only. Indeed, the road reopened the next morning, though I am unclear why. To the right of our car, fires were burning up the slopes. To our left, helicopters dipped giant buckets in the river. And directly in front, brigades of weary firefighters reconnoitered.

We had no idea ours would be the last vehicles to get through for some time. Ignorant, happy fools, off we went.

On the second morning, the river looked different. Leafy bric-a-brac floated by, followed by branches, then logs, then sludge. The Salmon was metamorphosing into a debris-choked, belching mass of chocolate pudding. Way upstream, creek drainages stripped of slope-holding vegetation by the fire had blown out with a thunderstorm the night before and dumped massive amounts of mud and charred detritus into the river.

We shoved off into the muck since we had our miles to make come hell or high water. With no white left in the whitewater, every rapid was dark and threatening. Soon our clothes, teeth and boats took on a murkish, tar-like hue.

A burst of thunder proclaimed a new round of sleety rain, howling winds and lightning bolts. While husband Bill wrestled the rain tarps, I passed around trail mix to the cold, hungry kids. Our one highly allergic, asthmatic member discovered a new nut to add to her no-no list, and she quickly slumped into a full-blown anaphylactic reaction.

Then our luck turned. Sunny skies, good runs through the rapids and no more nuts, of any kind. We settled into the comfortable routine we had come for: beautiful summer days and starry nights around the campfire, playing with the river and howling at the moon, talking deep philosophy, or nonsense, as the mood struck.

By Day 7, our travails were only a memory. We had snagged one of the most prized campsites and pulled in early enough to enjoy a full afternoon of play. Each of us was yearning for time in and around this site's namesake, California Creek. After a week in the Salmon's dirty water, we relished the clarity and crisp chill of this stream.

"Doesn't get any better than this, yah?" sighed Bill, as we lounged by the side of the creek, our legs cooling in the water.

"Mind if I join you?" asked our teenage son Greg as he hopped atop a boulder to my left.

It was only because Bill happened to be looking beyond me to the boulder, because it was such a uniquely shaped, mysteriously perched rock, that I wasn't squashed on that perfectly perfect afternoon. Spying a sudden shift of sand at its base, "MOOOVVVEEEE!" he bellowed. The boulder whacked my arm and Greg's leg as it launched him forward into the creek.

Our impromptu group medical staff, nurse Bill and EMT Beth, stabilized us with the help of a doctor they snagged off another group floating by. Greg soon sported an innovative splint contraption fashioned from paddles, a lounge chair and duct tape.

With the help of other river travelers, we sent an SOS for an emergency lift downriver from one of the small jet boats servicing the dude ranches. It was late afternoon and we were a day-and-a-half from our take-out and the nearest road.

The odor of gas and stale beer announced the arrival

of Mike, his battered jet boat and co-pilot Bubba. Mike kicked aside the empty beer cans littering the boat's floor, and hauled the three of us in. Then he and Bubba popped two fresh ones and our rescue craft took off in a belch of fumes and smoke. We roared downriver like a riderless jetski, tilting back and forth at 45-degree angles and flying up into the air, only to slam back down. Mike steered with his right pinky and his left knee, and occasionally looked back at us with a crooked grin as if to say, 'Y'all havin' fun?' Greg was in a happy Vicodin haze so he smiled back and gave him a thumbs up.

We arrived at take-out a mere 12 minutes later, Bill calculating that we had been traveling at 50 mph. Stopping just short of Vinegar Creek Rapid, one of the river's most feared, Mike chuckled. "Don't wanna try that one with the sun in me eyes," having maneuvered this far by instinct, memory and beer.

While Bill jumped out and ran for our car, Mike and Bubba both dropped their drawers and peed into the river. Bill returned. Our car was not there. (We later learned that the mudslide that flooded the river earlier in our trip had also trapped our cars at put-in.) Bill brokered a deal with a guy and his station wagon to drive the three of us into the small town of Riggins, where an ambulance took everyone to a larger town with an emergency room.

Our new rescuer backed his car down the steep ramp to load the immobile Greg, Bill and me, popped the clutch and almost rolled us all off a steep drop back into the river.

The ambulance ride was neat, especially when a herd of elk crossed the highway in our path as we toodled along at 85 mph. But Frank, the driver, possessed amazing powers (and loads of experience) dodging herd animals at twilight and we made it to the ER in one piece.

Greg and I were bandaged up and our party made it home in plenty of time to begin working on applications for next year's lottery, hoping once again to win the golden ticket. We have a matter to settle with a certain boulder. And I want to pass along a six-pack to our buddy Mike.

The Khaki Pants

by Kristi Porter

ON A TWO-WEEK VACATION OVER SPRING BREAK, my husband, Dennis, was driving our new conversion van when he swerved to avoid a large hole in the road. The front tires missed the hole but the rear tires scored a direct hit.

About an hour later Dennis began complaining about a shimmy in the rear tires. We got off at the next exit, Ocala, Florida, and found a tire company to do the necessary re-alignment. After lunch with our son, Andy, 12, and nephew, AJ, 13, we picked up the car and resumed our journey.

We didn't get very far. Suddenly, the car lurched. I heard the sound of crunching fenders, grinding metal and squealing tires. The van slid to a stop. Thinking we had been hit, Dennis checked to make sure everyone was all right and then got out of the van to discover the driver's side rear wheel gone. The van sat on nothing more than the axle, which had carved a two-inch groove into the pavement. Gasoline slowly leaked from the punctured fuel tank.

Witnesses told us that the wheel had just "jumped" off the van and careened across seven lanes of traffic. The local fire department washed away the spilled fuel, and our van was loaded onto a flatbed wrecker and taken to a local dealer. The mechanic looked at it, made a long, slow whistle, and said he could probably have us mechanically back on the road in four or five days, but if we wanted the body damage repaired, we were looking at two weeks. I told him to make it run, and our family would take care of the cosmetic problems on our return to Michigan.

I called a car rental company, and they arrived to pick us up in a Chrysler Sebring convertible—top down. My husband announced that this was the car he wanted to rent until our van was ready. The rental agent said, "No problem, just sign here," and handed us the keys.

Back at the dealership, we loaded our luggage and other bags into the convertible and headed to our campground, about 10 miles away. On the way there was a tropical downpour. Of course none of us had any idea how to put the top back up. Five minutes later, parked on the side of the road and soaking wet, we finally figured it out.

The next morning, after spending two hours on the phone with the dealership, insurance company and tire company in Ocala, (which had failed to properly tighten the wheel after the alignment) we visited Disney World.

The Raging Rivers ride sounded like fun. Everyone was instructed to place their valuables in a waterproof center compartment, and my husband dutifully placed our cell phone inside. Partway through the ride the top of the compartment came unlatched and our cell phone, which had been on top of the other items, bounced out and onto the floor where it sat in several inches of water until the ride ended. It was fried.

Four days later I picked up our mechanically sound, but awful-looking van, and headed back to the tire company in Ocala. The rear bumper was nestled between the seats, and other assorted fenders and parts were stashed throughout the van. After hours discussing liability with corporate management at the tire company, we checked into a local campground and went out for a late dinner.

It was well after dark when we returned to our cabin, all of us tired and cranky. As my husband reached for the light switch, he felt something brush against his hand. A large, red, black and yellow snake was curled around the switch box and electrical conduit. It slowly slid into a hole in the wall just as the light bulb popped, leaving the cabin in darkness. The kids made a mad dash to the campground office, while my husband and I watched in the dark for the snake to return.

The campground manager was awakened, and he arrived with a picture book of snakes, asking us to identify what we had seen. Not being familiar with Florida wildlife, we weren't sure, but it looked like a King snake. Since no other cabins were available, the campground sent us to a motel across the street at their expense. Since none of us wanted to return to the dark cabin, we moved with only the clothes on our back. The following morning our family checked out, retrieved our belongings from the cabin and drove to our original destination, Lake Okeechobee.

The first two days were wonderful. The cabin was great, the weather was perfect, and I began to think that this was not going to turn out to be a National Lampoon vacation. The third day my husband developed an itchy rash on his hand, and he made a trip to the local pharmacy for some ointment. By evening the rash had spread to his arms, legs and chest, and he headed to the nearby medi-center, which did not accept our medical insurance.

The doctor said the itch probably was an allergic reaction to something, and gave my husband a prescription for Benadryl and an anti-itch cream. Three pharmacies later, he found one that would accept our medical insurance, got the medication and went back to the campground. The next morning I woke up with the same rash on my legs and stomach. By evening the kids were also itching badly.

The following morning we packed up and headed north to Bradenton, planning to stop and visit friends for a day or so before heading home. They looked at our rashes and recommended a local physician. He looked us over, asked several questions about our trip and announced we had a severe case of bedbugs.

I learned that bedbugs can live in mattresses and burrow under the skin of victims and lay eggs, which hatch about 48 hours later, causing a rash and intense itching. The cure was to be covered in a thick prescription cream from head to toe before bed for three consecutive nights and rinse the cream off with a hot shower every morning. Every piece of clothing must be washed, in the hottest water possible. All bedding must also be washed, daily, during the course of treatment, or risk re-infection. I filled his prescription and we spent the next day in our swimsuits, doing laundry.

Two days later, in Indiana, our vehicle was sidelined by another flat tire. After putting on the spare and buying a new tire, we drove into a snowstorm. It was the perfect end to our spring vacation that was nearly over. Suddenly my husband, worried about the way the car was handling, eased the van onto the shoulder of the road and stopped. There was a thud and the right rear of the van felt like it was dropping into a hole. We all looked silently at each other, then got out of the car.

The tire in question was fully inflated. Unfortunately it had fallen off and was lying on the pavement, pinned beneath the van. We were only 50 miles from home, stranded and without a cell phone, in what was to become one of the biggest snowstorms of the season. Luckily, a passing motorist stopped and let us use his cell phone to call a wrecker. Due to the snowstorm it would be at least an hour before they got to us.

After several minutes of silence, AJ said he thought maybe his khaki pants were cursed. Looking at the rest of us huddled in the van, he pointed out that everything bad on this vacation had happened while he was wearing his khaki pants. He had even slept in them the night we stayed for free in the bedbug motel. It was just a coincidence, I assured him. It had to be.

The wrecker finally arrived two hours later and loaded the van onto the flatbed. A cab would take us on the final 50 miles of our journey. As the driver prepared to pull into traffic, AJ screamed at him to wait. He wanted to change out of his khakis, just in case. Denny hoisted AJ onto the flatbed, handed him the keys, and told him to hurry. AJ climbed into the van, changed into his sweat pants, and tossed the khakis into the back of the van.

The cab driver ferried us home while the tow truck headed to a garage with our van. The Porters would retrieve their things from the van the following day. With the wind howling and snow swirling around us, we stood outside the back door of our North Muskegon, Michigan, home, as Denny searched his pockets for the keys. Then, remembering that he had given the keys to AJ, he squeezed his eyes shut and shook his head. The keys were in the van, in the pocket of AJ's troubled khaki pants.

Locked out of the house, we stood shivering in the dark while Denny smashed a window to get in. Once inside, we vowed that khaki pants would no longer be allowed on any vacations.

The following day the window was fixed, and the cell

phone was replaced. My husband retrieved our belongings from the van, which was repaired a week later, and then sold at a considerable loss.

The khaki pants were burned.

And to this day, whenever something goes wrong, the first question anyone asks is, "All right, who's wearing khaki?"

Crash Course in Spanish

by Tina Martin

I'D BEEN BACK FROM CHILE FOR ONLY A FEW HOURS when a nice policeman pulled me over for making a "California Stop," which is not quite a stop, and wrote out a bonus ticket because I didn't have my driver's license with me.

"It was in my wallet, which was stolen a couple of days ago . . . 8,000 miles away in South America," I told him. I was waiting for him to respond, "Yeah, that's what they all say," but he just politely handed me my tickets and commented that he was trying to brush up on his Spanish. Even though he hadn't exactly asked, I made the usual recommendations like watching *People's Court* and *LA Law* in Spanish or marrying someone who needed a green card. But I forgot to mention the method that had led to the second ticket he was giving me: Getting robbed on the metro in a Spanish-speaking country.

As a Christmas/graduation gift for my son in December 2001 after travel prices had been slashed following the attacks on the World Trade Center, I offered him a trip anyplace in the world—*with his mother.* My son chose Chile, where we had friends, one of whom had been a political prisoner for the three years following General Augusto Pinochet's coup on September 11, 1973. I mention this because the subject became part of my Spanish lesson.

Our friends in Chile were among those who advised me not to get robbed.

"If someone stops to ask you something, pretend that you don't speak Spanish," one friend told me, "and just move on."

"That's no fun!" I said. Practicing my Spanish was high on my list of things to do in Chile, no matter how much it obfuscated communication. (*Como se dice eschew obfuscation en español?*)

Maybe I was too old to do what I'd done in Madrid almost 30 years earlier. Then, fresh out of the Peace Corps (and with my Peace Corps Readjustment Allowance of $1,500), I'd gone to Spain and almost immediately headed for the University of Madrid to make some friends—preferably a boyfriend—who would be willing to speak Spanish with me. Finding the campus deserted, I realized that it was *Semana Santa*—Holy Week—and the campus was closed. But just as I was murmuring something stronger than *caramba,* I spotted a handsome bearded man who was checking job announcements on the bulletin board, and we met, spoke, exchanged numbers, met again, fell in love and spent a year of evenings in Madrid sharing *vino tinto* and *tapas,* singing in *mesones* and spending weekends by the fireplace in Peguerinos. That's how I'd improved my Spanish back then.

But now, in my 50s, if I appeared in a university *corredor,* I would be taken for a professor instead of taken for *tapas.* Getting robbed, on the other hand, availed itself to travelers of any age. Besides, as perfect as my Spanish boyfriend was, he never gave me a document like the one I got from the *Prefectura de Radiopatrullas* in the *Metro Estación Baquedano* in Santiago, Chile, after I was robbed.

There was a certain irony in how I became a victim. I was robbed right after trying to warn another passenger of the same danger! My son even suspects that the passenger I tried to warn was the one who robbed me or at least set me up. She had boarded with a friend and fallen backward against my son, who noticed that her backpack was opened, putting her cell phone in clear sight and up for grabs. He wanted to warn her but didn't know Spanish for backpack. I knew it probably wasn't *paco de baco,* but I couldn't remember *mochila.* Now I'll always remember it because I think it was when her *mochila* caused her loss of balance that our attention was diverted away from my bag, which had someone else's full attention.

"My wallet's gone!" I cried after we jumped off at the next metro stop and I noticed my bag felt lighter. "After all the warnings! I've proven myself to be as stupid as they thought I was."

Instead of delivering the verbal punishment most parents receive on such occasions, my son tried to reassure me.

"It wasn't your stupidity. It was their . . . deftness," he said. "We still have my ATM card, so we can get more money. What did you have in your wallet?"

"My Visa. My ATM card. The card-key to our hotel room."

"That has the address and room number on it. We'd better call the hotel and tell them."

I had a good chance to practice my Spanish by explaining to a guard what had happened, leaving out the *paco de baco* part. Sweetly sympathetic, perhaps to my loss as well as to my Spanish, he obtained a special key and led us downstairs to a little room with a phone. We called the hotel, and I practiced declaring what a fool I was. (" *Que cabeza la mía!*") Then I had a chance to practice following directions, which I can't even do in English. We were to go to the metro station Baquedano. Thanks mostly to my son, who doesn't speak a word of Spanish, we got there. That's where I began my really intensive language course in Spanish.

Starting with the essential details—my age and my marital status—a young officer took down all the facts longhand in a ledger. I practiced words like *licencia de conducir del estado de* California, *Tarjeta Visa del banco* Working Assets, *Tarjeta* ATM, *Tarjeta de Salud* Kaiser, *fotos familiares, seguro automotriz de la compania de seguros CSSA* and *sesenta mil pesos en dinero efectivo* (60,000 pesos in cash). After an hour interview, he re-checked the facts with me as he put the final report into their computer. Then he printed out the report and sent a colleague off to get it stamped.

While we waited for the return of the document, I looked around and asked about the framed *Derechos de los Detenidos* (Rights of the Detained) on the wall, which led to a cultural exchange of sorts. He noted that protecting the rights of detainees was now a concern in the United States because the September 11 attacks had led to people being taken away without charges. Then he asked where we were headed when I was robbed. "Al museo de Allende," I replied. He'd never heard of it, and didn't seem to know anything about Salvador Allende, the elected president deposed by Pinochet. But the posting of the *Derechos de los Detenidos* indicated that he knew Pinochet was no longer in power.

Eventually the document came back signed with a

flourish and sealed with a very official blue stamp saying Carabineros de Chile, Santiago. No certificate of course completion could have thrilled me more than this official documentation of what I no longer had and when I stopped having it, all in Spanish! As I slipped the precious souvenir into my bag, the young officer commented, " *Usted es una en un millón!*" ("You're one in a million.") He explained that foreigners almost never reported robberies to the Chilean authorities. I translated this for my son, who wanted to know where foreigners did report crimes. The answer, of course, was to their embassies.

We headed to the American Embassy, referred to by Chileans who guided us along our way as *la fortaleza* (the fort). It did not look like a structure built on trust. *La fortaleza* brought back the 1982 movie with Jack Lemon and Sissy Spacek, *Missing*, based on the real disappearance of an American journalist who saw too much of the United States' complicity in the 1973 overthrow of Allende, an overthrow that took place on September 11 of that year. That explained some street signs saying *11 de septiembre.*

I assumed that everyone at the embassy would speak English too well to tolerate my Spanish, but I was *equivocada* (mistaken). They temporarily took my son's camera away from him and X-rayed my bag, proving that my wallet was, indeed, missing. Then, when we walked in through the very heavy doors, we found ourselves alone with someone who spoke English much, much too well for me to subject him to my Spanish. This turned out to be a recess from my Intensive Spanish Course. After calling the numbers he provided to block my Visa and ATM, we left that part of the fort and went back to get my son's camera.

" *Y ahora podemos tomar una foto de la fortaleza al*

exterior?" (And now can we take a picture of the outside of the fort?) I asked the guards, who replied, *"De ninguna manera."* ("No way.")

Our trip had things to recommend it besides my being robbed. Staying with friends in Algarrobo by the beautiful ocean, taking a friend's guided tour of Pablo Neruda's house at Isla Negra, staying in La Gran Palace above a cineplex showing *Harry Potter, El señor de los anillos, Los diarios de una princesa,* and *Monsters, Inc.* and going to free concerts at the Teatro Municipal in Santigo, discovering the tradition of *Las Onces* (the afternoon tea named for the 11 letters of *aguardiente,* which isn't tea), ascending and descending the hills of Valparaiso, where we stayed at the Brighton Hotel, picture-perfect enough to be featured on a postcard.

However, there's no postcard that I'd trade for my *Copia Certificada de Constancia Estampada,* that stamped document representing Spanish language practice I'd have missed were it not for the fact that I'd been robbed. I'll always cherish it even though, as I observed once I was back committing traffic violations in San Francisco, police officers won't accept it as a substitute for a driver's license.

All Bets Are Off

by Dean G. Pappas

WHEN IT COMES TO TRAVEL, one destination always springs to the forefront of my mind. Whether for business or pleasure, the city that energizes me is the oasis in the desert, Las Vegas.

Whenever I can end up carousing in Sin City, gambling throughout the night as complimentary drinks flow endlessly, I embrace the opportunity. Each time I return to Chicago, I always have an interesting story to tell.

A few weeks before Christmas, my supervisor sent me to Las Vegas for a business trip. I would make the deal on Friday and have the weekend to immerse myself in Vegas' sleepless pace.

I let my friend of 15 years, Tim, know of my plans and suggested that he meet me there. Tim's brother worked for an airline, enabling Tim to fly for free. He could stay with me in my company-paid hotel room. This business trip would be an inexpensive vacation, barring major gambling losses.

After arriving in Las Vegas I quickly met my business contact and closed the deal. Returning to the hotel, I saw Tim, who had just arrived. Before long we were ready to go out into the electric night.

The newly opened Paris Hotel and Casino waited with its faux Eiffel Tower bathed in light. Tim and I entered the French-themed casino and moved through the sea of one-armed bandits toward a back wall lined with "Wheel of Fortune" slot machines. Nearly all of the machines had patrons feverishly feeding in money, pressing buttons and pulling levers. We sat down at two of the machines next to each other and began playing.

After about half an hour Tim turned to me and asked what would happen if three "Wheel of Fortune" symbols came up. I explained that the horizontal electronic sign above the row of machines displays numbers representing dollars. The numbers constantly increase reflecting a progressive jackpot connected throughout Nevada. Hit those three symbols and win the jackpot. Tim asked if the jackpot was in quarters. I indicated that there was a dollar sign in front of the number although 1.4 million quarters wouldn't be too bad either. Five minutes later I lined up symbols and won $200. Not bad. Tim and I high-fived and continued playing. Two minutes had passed when Tim's machine started flashing and ringing. He slapped me on the shoulder and pointed to the reel window.

There they were. Three "Wheel of Fortune" symbols in a row . . . $1.4 million.

Six security guards surrounded us. A casino representative approached and offered his congratulations. We posed for a photo with an oversized check. Tim, still in shock, went with me to a casino office.

For several hours, I reviewed paperwork for Tim, who had made me his spokesman. A check was presented to Tim for nearly $70,000 (with 19 more to follow in time), and a limousine provided to take us to Excalibur to retrieve our belongings. We were moving to a complimentary suite at Paris.

You might expect that two single guys in Vegas with a check for $70,000 (taxes weren't taken out) would find a way to enjoy themselves. Despite on-call limos, an amazing $5,000 per night suite and the casino's offer to cash all or part of the first check, Tim decided to remain his dour self.

Our post-win time in Vegas started out with excellent potential. As we entered the dark blue Lincoln limo six blonde women walked by. We invited them to join us and drove off to the Rio Hotel's 51st floor Voodoo lounge. But at the lounge, surrounded by six attractive girls, Tim refused to buy them as much as a Coke. When they realized that we weren't the high rollers they had hoped for, they all left.

Before long we also departed the bar in the sky. A little gambling followed, mostly my own. Apparently Tim was done for the trip. Another limo ride brought us back to Paris. Tim told me it was my turn to tip the driver. My turn? I looked at him and pulled out a ten. Day one was over. Maybe Saturday would be better.

We ate lunch at a little French café just off a bank of slot machines. Tim ordered me to call the waiter over for the check. I refused and said since we were comped he had to sign for it. Lunch ended, thankfully. I proceeded to play some slots, while Tim sat by watching and drinking a beer.

We scheduled massages at the hotel and spent an hour relaxing while being worked on by professional masseuses. The afternoon faded away and soon it would be time for another night on the town. Tim had called his dad in Chicago and invited him to join us. An invitation was also extended to his uncle and cousin in San Diego.

As we looked at a $1,200 leather jacket embroidered with the Paris logo on it, Tim contemplated asking for a comp. He was also thinking about instructing the hotel to send a limo to pick up his father at the airport. I explained that the hotel was providing a limo and suite hoping he would return some of his winnings to the casino. If he failed to gamble, the casino might pull back on some of the amenities they were providing. He reluctantly agreed to begin assuming the role of the Big Player.

That evening his family arrived and immediately requested margaritas. Tim ordered two pitchers from room service. Total cost: $95. When no one tipped the waiter I gave him $10. Then it was on to the posh restaurant located in the mock Eiffel Tower overlooking the strip.

When the bill came I was shocked. Over $900. What had these people ordered? Tim reviewed the tab and discovered that their bottle of wine was $350. I offered to pay my share, $35, but Tim said the hotel would cover it and we left.

The family retired back to the suite, while Tim and I headed out. The rest of the night went as follows: Take the limousine to a casino, where I gambled while Tim watched and played a little, called the car, headed to the next casino, and repeated the process. Most of the tips were, of course, mine.

By now, Las Vegas, which had been the epitome of fun and entertainment, felt like a prison. I was ready to escape. Fortunately, Tim announced on Sunday morning that we were returning home that afternoon.

I quickly packed my suitcase and urged Tim to pick up the pace. I left a tip for the maid and hurried to the elevators that would bring me another step closer to home. We exited the elevator into the crowded casino.

I stood next to the slot machines, waiting for Tim to check out. After a long delay he explained there was a problem. We were directed to an office and joined by a casino host. Tim and I owed the hotel money. The massages weren't covered. The phone bill was $300, and the Eiffel Tower restaurant was operated by an independent party, not the hotel. The extravagant dinner was not complementary. We were presented with a bill.

Tim, slouched in his chair, rudely let the host know that he was a big winner. The man looked at his computer screen to see how much gambling we'd done during our stay. It wasn't much.

The employee excused himself and went to try and contact the Friday night host who had been on hand when Tim won his jackpot. Tim told me to handle the situation. With our flight leaving shortly, I decided to take over. I politely discussed our options. The host, as a gesture, eliminated the massages from the bill, which left a $1,300 tab. Tim still didn't want to pay. A free flight, a $1.4 million jackpot, luxurious accommodations and limousines at our disposal, and he was bothered by a small balance. The host finally decided that the problem could be resolved later through a telephone call with the original casino host. I thanked him and bolted for the taxi line.

As we waited for a cab, Tim reviewed the statement and told me that I owed $150 toward the phone charge. A minute later, a cab pulled up. I told the driver to get to the airport as fast as possible.

At the airport, Tim told me to pay the cab driver because "all I have are hundreds."

"I don't think so. This is Vegas, they'll break the hundred. *You* pay him." He did.

A week after our return, Tim got drunk, lost his temper in a bar, picked a fight with my brother and then backed down because "I'm a millionaire and don't want to get sued." As I drove him home that night, Tim passed out in my car. I escorted him to his house, closed the door and left.

I never saw him again.

Bare Boating

by Ellen Rubenson

IN JULY 1989, I EMBARKED ON THE DREAM OF A LIFETIME, a bare-boat charter in the Caribbean, destination the British Virgin Islands. "Bare" as in "No Crew." We were a motley foursome: myself, my husband Dan, friend Ellison and his then girlfriend, Cheryl.

Earlier in the year, we had sent our sailing resumes, such as they were, to the charter company. Ellison's experience was vast; Dan and I had sailed some in Hawaii and been on two other bare-boats. This was Cheryl's first sailing trip. Our boat was a Nelson/Marek 45 Morgan racing sloop, the Standfast II. Eager to sail, but remaining respectfully alert during the charter company's required orientation, our group made notes during a detailed description of the yacht's interconnecting systems. It was, of course, vital to know how everything works and where everything is stored, like the flotation cushions tucked neatly under the deck seats, a life ring snapped onto a railing on deck, the VHF radio in the galley and the two fire extinguishers in easy-to-release brackets below deck.

The charter company supplied two weeks' worth of food, a cruising guide with charts and navigation tools, motorized dinghy, barbecue grill and bikini top and sent us off with best wishes for a relaxing sail. We dubbed Ellison captain and left the harbor to the sound of his deep

Southern baritone booming out commands. "Prepare to unclip from the mooring. Dan to the mainsail; Ellen and Cheryl to the jib."

The weather looked like it had been arranged by the local tourist board. I found a piece of rock that appeared suited for underwater protection and named it a "shark bonker." But the first shark I identified was not a candidate for the bonker. After some speculation, I was able to identify it from a fish identification book as a filter-feeding shark, a fish that sucks plankton, small fish and fish eggs, separating them from the seawater with thousands of bristly gill rakers.

On our fourth day, we motored toward Drake Channel for a day of "just good sailing." Under a cloudless sky a few minutes after noon and only half a mile from the Tortola shoreline, Cheryl calmly said, "Is that smoke?" It was. Dense plumes were billowing up the stairs of the hatch from below deck. When Ellison and Dan opened the engine compartment, flames leapt out. They closed the compartment and went for the fire extinguishers. Ellison is a large man—6 feet, 3 inches, 220 pounds—and pulled the extinguisher off the wall, brackets and all. Dan released the safety latch on the second extinguisher, and the men emptied both into the crackling, fully engaged fire. But the flames from the engine roared out with new life and licked across Dan's legs as he fled to safety.

"Abandon ship!" Captain Ellison roared. He sailed away from the shoreline, where the dry brush and trees could easily ignite. Dan froze momentarily. Ellison grabbed his shocked mate's arm and got him moving. Dan helped Cheryl pull the dinghy in while I kept the sloop steady. We crawled one by one into the dinghy, fearful the propane tanks on the Standfast II would explode at any moment. When Dan pulled the cord, the dinghy engine started, then stalled. We failed to notice the painter line wrapped around the propeller. The dinghy drifted to safety, surrounded by yachts and cruisers drawn by the fire. Dense smoke and orange flames were curling above deck.

In the distance, the management at Frenchman's Cay Resort on Tortola was standing on the white sand beach, beckoning us to their island. They offered towels and asked what they could get us to drink. Wrapped in towels and sipping vodka tonics, the resort guests joined us to watch the fire department pump water into the hull of the Standfast until she sank 65 feet to the ocean floor along with our clothes, money, passports, identification, airline tickets and a week's worth of food.

The charter company arrived promptly. Once they determined there were no injuries aside from Dan's hairless legs, our party was turned over to the police who were far from friendly. The gendarmes insisted we come to the station, separated Cheryl and I from the men and took us into back rooms to give our statements before releasing everyone an hour later to the charter company staff. Escorted to the hotel gift shop, our crew soon emerged with modest new wardrobes.

The company provided us with a replacement yacht, the Largo Bay, that we sailed into the path of Hurricane Dean. Our previous boat, the Standfast, would have ripped through the 10-foot swells. In the Largo Bay, we grunted and cursed the lack of control as it floundered through the looming waves. And then, the hurricane turned west, sprinkling us with just a light drizzle.

Sometimes you get lucky.

The Road to Somewhere

by Lisa Thompson

THE TRIP FROM THE BEACH TO TAPALPA, a little mountain town outside of Guadalajara, shouldn't take much longer than three hours. But the trip we'd begun that morning was unending.

I was lying in the rear third of the Explorer, scrunched between backpacks and hang-gliding harnesses. Luke wasn't talking. He'd stopped being friendly within a few minutes of our departure when he caught me looking scared on one of his kamikaze passes on a blind hairpin turn between our village and the highway. In the first months of our relationship, by being compliant and worshipful, I'd implicitly bound myself to a lifetime of necessary good-naturedness. Any unhappy looks crossing my face were a direct affront to the delicate balance of our lives, a threat to unhinge the perfect world we'd created at the edge of the jungle, under the palapa. How could I suddenly begin to object to things that I'd previously encouraged without betraying a stunning lack of character—revealing myself to have loved, but not to have known what I loved?

I let my guard down. I showed fear and disapproval. It all went downhill from there.

He swore he knew the way. He'd been there so many times before, back in the good old days.

We took the scenic route, coming up on Guadalajara from the southwest. It might have been easy. We could

34

have had cross words on the trip, but had we gotten there within a reasonable margin of error from three hours, we could have recovered. But he couldn't find the town. The map wasn't helping. Stopping for directions didn't help. Stopping for directions in Mexico is famously not a productive solution and believe me, that is no myth. Like me, Mexicans don't like to say no. It's not polite. They will happily give directions to anywhere—smiling, elaborating, pointing—whether or not they know where it is, or have ever heard of it.

The cobblestone streets of one narrow town were filled with a parade of some sort. I don't remember seeing a saint, but the growing pain in my back, my hunger, my fear that we were never going to stop to eat, my seething resentment that I had no control over these things produced a Fellini-esque quality to the scenes outside the window. Faces would grow larger, cheering as we drove through town, then leer as we zoomed past them a second time, hopelessly circling even this small pueblo.

Just after dark Luke pulled over to the side of the road, climbed into the middle seat with his dog, and went to sleep without a word.

Trying to keep my voice steady, I inquired about the possibility of dinner. He replied angrily, not really answering the question, just letting me know that dinner was not an option—we were driving no further. I whimpered to myself. I was freezing and my back was getting worse with the cold. I tried to be quiet, but not so quiet that he wouldn't notice me getting out of the car, calling my dog and walking back and forth down the dark road. I couldn't go far. There was nowhere to go. It was dark. I had no vehicle and I was somewhere in Jalisco. Who knew where.

I paced. Down the road as far as I dared, then back again. I tried to be calm. I tried to get warm. I got back in the truck and started it up. I'm going to drive for awhile, I explained calmly. We need to eat, and maybe I can find a room to stay in, some directions, something. I drove awhile. Soon I found an open taco stand and parked trucks scattered about. At least we were on a major route. The dogs and I got out. I ordered tacos for us, relieved with my small victory. I had wrested control and now we were eating. We could still make Tapalpa that night.

When I got back to the truck he was behind the wheel. He cursed me for my selfishness, for causing him excruciating pain while he suffered from a migraine. Well, that came as a shock. Why hadn't he told me he had a migraine? If I'd known, I could have given him some of that forgiveness I was famous for. He found a dark spot off the road that led away from the taco stand and pulled off. I put on as many clothes as I had with me, curled up with my dog and did my best to sleep.

In the morning he was slightly less afflicted and angry. We ate at a gas station, Bimbo brand powdered donuts and instant coffee, if I remember correctly. The road I'd inadvertently found in the night was just the one he'd meant to be on. We were in a broad, dry valley, with the volcanoes of Colima to the south and Guadalajara to the northeast. The mountains of Tapalpa lay just ahead. We made town within an hour and checked into a hotel just across from the *zócalo*. From outside it looked like an old western saloon; you could easily imagine the upstairs balcony filled with bordello girls. Most of what I remember about the days of staying there was darkness. Luke still had the migraine, and he stayed in bed in the room with the curtains drawn for the next several days.

I roamed the town. I'd spent several years by then in Mexico but hadn't gone into the interior much, so most of what I knew of life there was learned on the tropical coast. I was unprepared for the ponderosa beauty of this mountain town, with its thick walls and dark, wooden doors, its steep streets and cold nights. I bought long pants and a sarape, then sought out a homeopath for back medicine. I bought presents for family; I wrote in a café on the *zócalo,* and I made friends with a man named Juan Pablo.

I met him on that first day of exploring. He was blond, quiet, elegantly polite. He lived on a ranchero outside of town, and had come in that morning to bring some produce to the grocery store and to pick up supplies. I was interested then in importing bicycles, and he offered to take me to meet a friend of his who ran a bike store in town. I can't remember what we talked about that day, but I clearly remember feeling that I could return to Tapalpa later, and find him waiting, holding a door open for me.

That night in our room, a new nightmare. I was curled up in my particular twin bed on an old mattresss, trying to sleep. Some young men, drunk with booze and life, were somewhere in town below us singing. First one song, and then another, followed by laughter, jovial yelling, howling and more song.

I cherished those moments: surprises offered from an enduring culture—not mine by birth, but by choice. To hear men singing together in the street was beautiful to me.

But a man with a migraine feels differently. Luke made a stand, just like an imaginary *Gunsmoke* hero might have done, from the picturesque balcony. He cursed the men, threatened them, yelled that they were lousy singers.

The next day Luke stayed in bed again. I walked to the café and Juan Pablo pulled up next to me. We went for another drive in his VW bus. We walked amongst some ruins outside of town, a bright field with a stream, elegant rocks and a sky filled with bluebirds. The rocks were golden and tall—they could be climbed—and they cast shadows that stretched and bent across the grasses in the field. I looked out across that meadow, smelled the pine mountain air and imagined that I could see all throughout Mexico from that spot. From here the coast seemed childish and dirty, pinned together with palm fronds and four-hour work days, slow and lazy from too much heat, decaying and vapid from the encroaching jungle, a Mexico that I knew but which I suddenly despised as one regrets the mean self left behind after adolescence, after growing up.

Returning to town I saw an old man with a burro outside our hotel. He and the burro were old and solid. The old man purchased an ice from the young boy who sold them each day in the sun. The burro wore a beautiful blanket of many colors—bright Mexican colors. I took a picture of the burro. I took a picture that I knew would remind me of this time later, when a high mountain zócalo would seem very far away.

That evening, I went to the store and closed the door to the phone behind me. I called my brother and told him I was coming home.

Exotic Egypt

by Seymour Collins

IT ALL TOOK PLACE IN EGYPT during the 1990 Christmas season.

"Let's not go," my wife, Annie, said. "There's going to be a war. It's just not safe for Americans to travel in that part of the world."

"Nonsense," I responded. "Besides, we can't pass up this opportunity. Our friends are letting us use their apartment in Cairo for a week, and then we'll go up the Nile and see all the great sights just like we've been planning. Nothing will happen."

Morgan met us in his Suzuki at about 3 a.m. outside the Cairo airport and drove us, wheels straddling the lane stripes, along an almost deserted highway toward their apartment. In the year that he and Linda had been living and working in Cairo, he had apparently learned the local customs. We noticed that he didn't pay any attention to traffic signals either.

We fell asleep almost immediately upon reaching the apartment and were awakened several hours later by prayer calls emanating from nearby mosques along with incessant automobile horns. From our ninth-floor apartment window we could see that we were located on an island in the Nile, its banks lined with houseboats.

Our friends instructed us on life in Cairo. "Here's how to contact Kamal, the taxi driver. He can take you to the

Khan el-Khalili Bazaar. Around the corner is a bakery; you can buy a real papyrus from a dealer down the street; the fruit and vegetable market is on the next block; be sure to wash all food in bottled or boiled water; *La* means no; *Aiwa* means yes. If you make an appointment with someone he will invariably respond with *inshallah*, as God wills. If he doesn't show up then God just didn't will it. *Mish mumkin* means not possible and is rarely used by anyone trying to sell you something. More likely you will hear *mish mushkilla*, no problem. Got it? Here are the keys to the front door." And then they were gone.

I said to Annie, "Maybe we'll get through this."

She said, "*Inshallah.*"

Cairo, a huge metropolis by any standard of measurement, had in the few weeks prior to our visit added some 1 million people to its population bringing the total to, some said, about 16 million. The increase was attributed to the return of Egyptian workers from threatened Kuwait. We had thought that there might be some antagonism to Americans because of the impending war, but that isn't what we experienced. What we heard was, "We love George Bush! Saddam Hussein, he's a madman! Come and see my papyrus. Merry Christmas!"

It would be uncivilized for a first-time visitor to not visit the ancient tombs, and there is no end to the number of tombs to visit. One of the tombs in Saqqara, just a bit south of Cairo, was made especially interesting by a guide who seemed as old as the tomb itself. He explained that some of the mummy's organs were placed in canopic jars and buried in separate compartments within the tomb. "In this tomb," he said, "the stomach is 30 meters down! Do you understand me? Thirty meters down!" He said it with such vehemence while vigorously pointing downward that neither Annie nor I were about to ask him to convert that to feet. We gave him some baksheesh and left.

On another day we visited the Sphinx and the Great Pyramids at Giza. Maybe we were tempting fate for this is where Alexander once stood, and Caesar and he each met premature deaths. Nonetheless, we explored the interior of the Pyramid of Chephren and even got to enter the tomb chamber, where I was either bold or dumb enough to crawl into the open sarcophagus for a photo opportunity. "Are you nuts?" Annie yelled.

"It's just an inanimate old stone box," I said. "It has no power. At least, not after all these years."

Now I'm not so sure.

After a week spent absorbing the culture and seeing the sights in Cairo, we flew south to Luxor to begin our cruise up the Nile. Maybe that's where it happened. The Nile. The River of Life. In its unboiled waters, farm animals bathe alongside little children as shadoofs lift the almost viscous liquid to irrigate fields as they have been doing for time out of mind. On board our ship we met a couple; the man, an Egyptian of some official prominence in Cairo, and the woman, a beautiful Syrian reported by her husband to have been related to royalty. They had their two personable little sons with them and Annie couldn't resist remarking on how nice and well-behaved they were. Later we had dinner with a couple of young Arab men who were on leave from military service. One of them asked Annie if she believed in the evil eye. She was non-committal, but he said that he believed. He explained that when you heap praise upon someone it is the equivalent of placing the evil eye upon that person. He had heard Annie complimenting

the little boys and now advised her of how it most likely was received by their parents. Culture shock! We had
eaten the enticing fruits on board, asking only now and
then whether they had been washed in boiled water, but we
never thought to boil our words.

More culture shock. In this preponderantly Muslim
country we were greeted everywhere by banners and people wishing us a Merry Christmas. Neither Annie nor I
ever considered ourselves arrogant or indifferent to the
concerns and customs of others. We tried to imagine a
group of Muslims on a riverboat cruise down the Missis-
sippi during the month of Ramadan. The thought that they
would have been greeted wherever they went by banners
and people wishing them a happy and successful month of
Ramadan was simply preposterous.

After the cruise, we returned to Luxor and then worked
our way over to Hurghada. While crossing the Eastern
Desert we stopped for rest and refreshments at a bleak
little town that looked like something out of West Texas.
It was there that I had a bottle of soda, pulled out by my
own hand, from an ice cooler. I drank the contents directly
from the bottle. I wish I hadn't done that. It's those little
things—things like the evil eye and boiled water and ir-
resistibly luscious figs and dates and impure chunks of ice
and the curse of a 4,500-year-old pharaoh—that you have
to be wary of in Egypt. And there is something else.

One day, with a small group of non-English speaking
tourists, we boated out to the coral shoals in the Red Sea
for a day of snorkeling. The coral and the fish were brilliant, prettier than any I had ever seen. I was so engrossed
in them that I failed to notice the reluctance and difficulty
that Annie had getting out of the boat and into the water.

She had removed her flippers because they were too awkward for her to handle, which led to her cutting her feet on the sharp coral. Her ill-fitting facemask was no help either, as she found herself gulping for air but swallowing water. Fortunately, some members of our party realized what was happening and fished her out of the water not a moment too soon. She was suffering from hypothermia while I had gone blithely on looking at colorful fish. It was only when we returned to our room that she poured out her story and I realized how close she had come to drowning. Maybe it was a case of sympathetic pains on my part or maybe I was just tired of having fun, but my arm and leg muscles felt sore and we both agreed to return home to the U.S. early.

Almost immediately upon arrival at our home in Oakland, California, the muscular aches and pains that I had noted became more pronounced, accompanied by alternating chills and fever at night. Soon I could not raise my arms above shoulder height and my leg muscles reduced my walk to a shuffle. I could not tie my shoelaces without assistance. Quite by happenstance, a routine physical examination which included a chest X-ray indicated spots or nodules on my lungs. The doctor couldn't be sure of their nature without a biopsy.

The operation was performed in October 1991, 10 months after we had returned from Egypt. The next day a cadre of specialists accompanied by the head nurse and an assistant janitor arrived with the news. I had contracted cryptococcus, a disease that would have been fatal 10 years earlier. *Mish mushkilla*—no problem.

I was lucky. Chemotherapy would take care of it—*inshallah*.

To this day, no one has determined what caused my

43

body to act so strangely. But my symptoms have almost disappeared, although I have noticed, on nights when the moon is full and aligned with the Pyramids of Chephren and Cheops in far-off Giza, a feeling as if bandages are being wrapped around my limbs and torso. I swear I can hear, "Thirty meters down. Do you understand me? Thirty meters down."

Victorino's Bar

by Li Miao

A PILGRIMAGE IS A JOURNEY OF FAITH, and the Camino de Santiago has challenged many a pilgrim with tortures of the body and tests of the soul for nearly 1,100 years. On a three-week journey with my fiancé, Andrew, our travails were often rather mundane—shielding our bodies from the relentless summer sun, struggling to understand the torrent of Castilian Spanish, scrounging for food during siesta hours when everything in Spain was closed.

While the wild cards of traveling weren't exactly a forecast of our future married life, we'd gotten on each other's nerves enough that we decided to spend a day apart.

I arrived in Hontanas at 3:30 in the afternoon. The first thing that caught my eye was the big Coca-Cola sign by Bar Victorino. Andrew's guidebook had warned against the cheap rooms and meals. I could find a better meal down the street at the *albergue*, or pilgrim's hostel. But the room above the bar looked decent, so I decided to park my dusty backpack and sore muscles there for the night. It would be around $12, a fraction of what we'd paid previously.

Downstairs in Victorino's bar, a cyclist pointed out something in his guidebook to Victorino and handed me his camera. As I clicked the shutter, Victorino began to pour a flask of red wine onto his ancient forehead. The burgundy liquid cascaded down to the tip of his nose, then into the cavern of his outstretched jaw. The guidebook had a crisp photo of Victorino—20 years younger—doing the same trick. And on the wall of the bar was a large portrait of the man with the same flask, perhaps decanting the same bottle of wine all these years. Something about Victorino's bar seemed as ancient as the sacred route to Santiago, yet tinged with staleness, like an old block of goat cheese that refuses to be thrown out.

Feeling a little stifled, I headed out in search of a bench in the shade. A man strolled by and sat down beside me. Gathering I was a pilgrim, he asked, "Are you traveling alone?" With Andrew in town staying at the *albergue* down the street, I tried to explain in my best Spanish that we were taking time apart to think and do our own thing.

"Where are you staying?" he asked. When I said I had a room in Victorino's bar, the man curled his nose. He went on at length and then said Victorino was *abusadivo* with a dismissive wave of his hands. The word rolled out like a tractor rumbling over the wheat fields. I asked him to repeat it, slowly. It seemed important enough not to miss.

"Wait," I said, as I looked the word up in my dictionary. *Abusadivo*. Excessive, e.g. in drinking. Takes advantage of. Since Victorino's prices were reasonable enough, I decided there may be some uncouth behaviors I might want to know about.

"Drinks too much?" I asked.

"No," the man replied. But he would not give away any of the town gossip. Or, perhaps, he was just envious of Victorino's fame.

As I got up to leave, I asked the man his name. It was Caesar, who owned the *casa rural* that I'd tried to phone earlier in the day without any luck. "Ay!" I remarked.

"If I'd been able to call you, I would have stayed at your inn."

Early in the evening I headed to the *albergue* for supper. Pilgrims came in steadily to dine, speaking Spanish, German, French and English, filling the exquisitely rustic room with a symphony of laughter and pilgrim lore.

When I got back to Victorino's bar at 9:30 p.m., he was alone in its dark cavern. The loneliness that filled the room was louder than the drone of the Spanish evening news. The fireplace against the back wall must have held secrets that smoldered in its dark bowels, flanked by a heap of broken-down boxes and rubbish, including a crumpled fistful of my lunch remains that I'd asked him earlier to throw out.

I wished him good night and made my way up the stairs, wondering if I would fall through its loose, wooden slats to the lonely abyss below. I was eager to take a shower and wash off two days of grime.

I twisted the hot and cold water knobs this way and that, lathered up and then discovered that the cold water would not shut off. I pushed the knob in further to turn it, but like the cranky threads of a medicine bottle, the knob turned aimlessly. Sensing some urgency, I quickly rinsed off my hair and got dressed. I knocked softly on the door to Victorino's room. No answer. "Victorino!" I cried, but my voice was engulfed by the shadows.

Determined to take care of the problem, I went back into the bathroom, and played with the cold water knob. Suddenly the knob fell off the fixture, and a horizontal pistol of cold water burst across the bathtub onto the hard wooden floor.

Now I was really in trouble. I kept forcing the knob

against the raging stream of water, to no avail. Then I discovered that the shower curtain could actually confine the jet of water inside the bathtub. A thin film of plastic would save me from the wrath and judgment of the townsfolk. "Those Chinese pilgrims, they're bad news," I could hear them say. "Those pilgrims, they drink too much and flood our houses."

My next move was to get help, and I made my way by flashlight down the creaky stairs since none of the light fixtures seemed to work. Outside, three older women were chatting. I quickly explained in broken Spanish, "The water in the shower, like a fountain . . . " I gesticulated and made a forceful whooshing sound.

I saw the Finnish pilgrim I'd met at supper and enlisted his help. He followed the beam of my flashlight up to the bathroom but was unable to reattach the knob against the stubborn jet of cold water. Meanwhile, the ladies had sounded out the alarm, and when a stocky man approached the bar, I explained as best as I could that we could not find the water main.

Now all hands were on deck. The village handyman got down on his knees and lifted three cement slabs off the sidewalk, stuck his arm into the hole and firmly wrenched the unseen valve shut. Upstairs the water stopped flowing, and the Finnish man easily screwed back the knob. Then, some villagers entered the dark kitchen downstairs. One turned on the faucet, flooding the room with an even bigger pool of water than the one in the bathroom. Gliding through the kitchen's puddle, I was able to shut that one off.

Everyone soon departed in a flurry of excited remarks that would be the town's big news of the week. I was left to clean the mess. I grabbed an old towel and found a bucket, threw out a shriveled piece of cured ham and got to work on the kitchen floor, mopping up a cocktail of cigarette ash, vinegar and oil, aged cheese, cheap liquor and the ghost of bread crumbs from the last two decades.

After I finished cleaning the bathroom, I lay in bed nursing my sore muscles and tired spirits. Twenty minutes later, I heard the rustle of the beaded curtain at the front door. It was now 11 in the evening. Victorino had returned. As I explained what happened, he looked around, finding only a wet bathmat and a newly polished kitchen floor. Strangely, the light fixtures and that cold water knob seemed to function for him. I said I needed to take a walk, to calm my nerves.

He wrapped his chubby arms around me and gave me a dozen hearty kisses on the cheeks. At 5 feet tall, I stood a forehead above his salty hair. The man had the square jaw of an ancient sailor and a torso like a barrel of sea rations. I gently pushed him away, and with a faint smile excused myself.

The cool of the evening soothed my spirits. Dogs were sleeping under the sidewalk benches. A bat flitted out from the eaves. The path to the highway became a black hole where the universe ended outside this village. As I turned back toward town, I stopped, awestruck. The church was bathed in a golden halo of light, like a museum centerpiece by one of the great Masters. Lingering in its shadows, I found a large pool into which one of the village fountains poured, and sat on the cement. The mental static melted, giving way to a sudden shiver, as I stared into the life-giving water. The church bell chimed twice for the half hour. I reluctantly got up to return to the bar.

Victorino had the television on again, and I bid him

good night once more. "I am going to sleep," I said.

"*Conmigo?*" With me? His cement jaw broke into a toothy grin.

"My spouse is in the *albergue*," I said, shaking a finger at him.

"You're a nice girl," he smiled.

"I'm your cleaning woman," I muttered. Back in my room, I latched the door solidly behind me and went to sleep.

The next morning, I paid up and said a perfunctory thanks to Victorino, who seemed rather stern and sullen. Passing the *albergue* down the street, I saw Andrew in the doorway. As we walked away, I told him about the near disaster in the bar and Victorino's advances. He was a harmless man, a lonely man. But Andrew was incensed, and a stormy funnel swept across his face. "I'm going to talk to the man," he said, throwing down his pack.

I waited by the trail, wondering if there would be a scene like a saloon fight in an old Western. When Andrew returned, he appeared calm and collected. No blood had been spilled, or red wine spit with venom across the forehead.

Are you Victorino? Don't you ever touch my woman again . . . I didn't do anything, really . . . You're a liar, and you know it.

"He didn't fight back," Andrew said, grinding his walking stick into the soft dirt. His anger, like a summer storm, had coursed through and passed.

My own flurry of emotions had also calmed, giving way from the frenzied torrent of the night before to a trickle of musings in the morning's soft breeze. Did I have grand visions about this pilgrimage? Perhaps, but I now realized that each step of the journey would be marked by humble lessons.

One: If the guidebook says steer clear, avoid a place like the plague. Two: You get what you pay for. And finally: For women who journey alone, beware of barmen who drink red wine off the tips of their noses. It takes a village to drown their sorrows.

Rembrandt's Mini Cruise

by Judy Paulsen

WHEN PEOPLE ASK ME FOR ADVICE about luxury cruising, they usually want to know about ports of call, dining possibilities, shore excursions, snorkeling and finding bargains. They really don't want to hear about my rocky cruise from Boston to Bermuda that took place between two hurricanes in the midst of the September 11 crisis. They certainly don't want to know about the December Eastern Caribbean cruise to three islands that had been wiped off our itinerary by a hurricane. And they don't even want to hear the story of our "fall foliage" cruise to New England. Actually, my husband and I arrived too early to see fall colors. But it was a good way to celebrate our anniversary and was half the price of similar cruises. Considering the fact that our vessel, the Rembrandt, had recently been the flagship of a famous cruise line, we knew we would travel in luxury.

This classic ship was spacious, the crew was great and the food was terrific. Along with 1,000 fellow passengers we saw the best of Maine and Nova Scotia including Bar Harbor, Peggy's Cove and Halifax. On the night of September 13, cruising from Nova Scotia to Quebec we took in a show and then headed for the dance floor. What a great way to celebrate our life together.

At 11:15 p.m. the captain went on the public address

system to extend the ambiance of our "pirate's night." We all laughed when he told us the ship was being "seized." Then he repeated himself. The details were hilarious. We were turning around and sailing back to Halifax where our ship would be immediately impounded. Everyone was ordered back to his or her cabins to begin packing. Suddenly the music ended, the drinks stopped flowing, food service ended and crew and passengers headed back to cabins as ordered. The joke was really on all of us.

At 5 a.m. we were all served our last breakfast and the ship arrived in Halifax where police cars lit up the dock with their gumball flashers. The authorities stormed our ship, seizing mattresses, kitchenware, dining tables, desks, musical instruments, paintings, roast beef, even coat hangers. By the time they finished several hours later all that was left were the ice cubes. After the vessel had been stripped, passengers were told they had 20 minutes to get off the ship. Thanks to their emergency training, the crew moved us off efficiently, just as if we had been hit by an iceberg.

Our cruise line had filed for bankruptcy and each of us struggled to find a way to return home. Some chose to fly back to the United States, others rented cars and a few were lucky enough to share cabins with strangers on The Big Road II, another vessel headed for New York. We chose to join a group of passengers squashed into seven vans that made the 13-hour trip across Nova Scotia and New Brunswick to Quebec City. When we arrived to begin our scheduled "shore excursions," news of our experience headlined local papers. "Passengers dumped on dock."

Entranced at Earthdance

by Pamela Alma Bass

THERE WAS A POINT IN MY LIFE when I wanted to be a hippie.
I mourned that I had been born too late for the '60s. I wore
tie-dye shirts covered with "no nukes" buttons. I mem-
orized all the songs from the musical "Hair." I swooned
over scruffy boys who reeked of pot. I was 13.

Now I am 33. I wear solid colors. I listen to classical
music. And I like my men clean-cut. Nevertheless, in the
wake of September 11, I found myself seeking comfort
in the arms of a stilt-walker named Stephen. Things were
going pretty smoothly until he invited me to Earthdance,
a techno-pagan camping festival for peace. I thought I'd
better go, because if I didn't he might dump me for some
hemp-wearing-hippy who thought Earthdance was the
next best thing after Burning Man.

Growing up in New York City I had seen the inside of a
tent exactly once, on the front lawn of our country house
in Mount Kisco when I was 7. Even this lasted only 10
minutes since I assumed the unfamiliar noises outside my
canvas walls came from tigers, rapists and men in plaid.
The fact that the Heinz Ketchup family mansion was
within running distance did not assuage my fears. My idea
of nature was a tree in a pot chained to the banister of a
building on Park Avenue.

Stephen said we were going to an Indian reservation,
so I envisioned Native Americans in colorful headdresses
doing rain dances to welcome us on their sacred land. I

dreamed of meeting a shaman who would tell us we were destined to be together forever. Later, I would make love to Stephen under the stars in front of the flickering flames of a campfire, while a budding Bob Dylan imitator played guitar and sang sad songs about the fate of the world.

Still, before agreeing to go, I barraged Stephen with pointed questions about the facilities to ease my lingering fear of squatting behind trees while Indian children aimed poisoned arrowheads at my descendant-of-pilgrims-behind. He swore there would be clean toilets, hot water and most important we would be together, close to the earth, basking in the majesty of nature. The only thing he was right about was that we were together and closer to the earth than one would have thought humanly possible.

Stephen went ahead of me to prepare the campsite for my impending arrival. On my drive north from San Francisco, gas-guzzling SUVs barreled past me sporting bumper stickers that commanded: "Nuke Bin Laden" and "Love Jesus." The lingering odor of fried foods and red meat wafted by as I drove past In-N-Out Burger. Billboards picturing dancing cows enticed me to drink country fresh milk. But I stayed my course. Somewhere past Santa Rosa the flurry of red, white and blue flags gave way to a series of crayoned signs showing me the road less traveled towards harmony, understanding, ecological correctness and my date.

Finally, my freshly bathed silver Volkswagen pulled into a barren dirt parking lot swarming with barefoot hippies and dance club hipsters who poured out of camper vans and bio-diesel vehicles trailing yoga mats, congo drums, homemade drug-smoking paraphernalia and children. Piercings proliferated through lips, navels, eyebrows and tongues. Thighs, backs and breasts blossomed with yin-yang symbols, butterflies and mandalas. There was nothing verdant in sight. As I stepped out of my air-conditioned vehicle the scorching heat enveloped me, making my clothes cling to me like new-and-improved Saran Wrap. A thick coat of dust invaded my nasal passages and coated my skin in a beige film. My allergies kicked in, transforming me from casually-sexy-camping-babe (a look that had taken hours to perfect) into sniveling, sneezing, snotty, red-nosed monster-girl destined to clutch wads of toilet paper for the remainder of the longest 24 hours of my life.

Stephen emerged from the haze of dust wide-eyed with excitement about the puppet show, the mandala making and the synchronized global meditation. I stood wide-eyed with horror contemplating my escape route.

"Sounds interesting," I said, throwing my arms around his firm, tattoo-free body in order to remind myself of why I had come.

To top it off there were no Native Americans in sight: no feather headdresses, no moccasins, no sweat lodges or shamans. There were only thousands of scantily clad hippie nymphets donning backless halter tops and midriff-flaunting tie-dye shirts, translucent mini-skirts, platform shoes and toe-rings. I considered an emergency shopping spree at the booths selling saris, sarongs, kangas, kafiyas, dashikis and tevas. I had packed practically, to show what a good camper I was. In khaki pants, a baggy T-shirt, and sneakers, I was the frumpiest yuppie at the festival.

Stephen guided me through a sea of tents explaining the ins and outs of tent-technology. There were three-room, all-weather, polyester tents tall enough to salute the sun in and wide enough to sleep six. There were tents with aluminum combi-poles, and two-door anti-mosquito mesh entryway flaps with reflective zipper pulls. There were quarter domes, half domes and super domes, which boasted leak-proof construction, extra floor cushioning, zip open skylights and built-in vestibules for added privacy. Then we came to Stephen's tent, your basic two-person tunnel number, dwarfed on all sides by skyscraper deluxe models.

"I bought you something," he said, fishing around in his backpack. My heart leapt in anticipation of my first gift, a clear sign that he was taking our relationship to the next level. From the plastic Walgreens' bag I extracted a red ski hat and a pair of wool gloves.

"I didn't want you to be cold tonight while you're sleeping," he said, wiping the sweat off his forehead. "But who wants to sleep anyhow with the reggae band promising to play 'All Night Long'?"

Not only did I hate reggae, but my insomnia-prevention routine also did not include pounding drums, neighboring political tent debates, unpredictable room temperatures and rocky bedding. "The best thing though, is that we are really close to Z's van, so we have our own living room!"

Z was Stephen's purple-haired 60-something friend who lived in a van decorated with Disney characters. Our "living room" was a couch with the stuffing spilling out of it.

"That's really creative," I said, because Stephen was cute and I wanted him to keep on kissing me.

I turned my nose up at the vendor offerings of seitan seaweed quinoa stew, soy smoothies and wheat grass shots, instead opting for an oversized bag of non-organic extra-salty tortilla chips, which I deemed safer. Shortly thereafter my hubris was punished by violent stomach cramps. My condition may have been aggravated by my refusal to drink water despite the record-breaking heat wave. Although I was parched, drinking led to peeing, and peeing led to the Porto-Potties that loomed liked enemy battalions across the wasteland.

My plan backfired, committing me to more time in those small–blue-death-contraptions than any human should have to endure. At first it was not so bad. But a few thousand hippies later, entering these doors of doom was like catapulting into a Dantean abyss. The lines were interminable. The toilet paper endangered. The soap and hot water became extinct. I multi-tasked: balancing one hand against the wall (careful not to touch any contaminated surfaces,) I held my pant cuffs off the floor, while attempting to squat a safe distance from the seat, hold my nose, avoid looking down, aim and relax. For a dark moment I contemplated where I could have been weekending if only my lust had led me into the arms of a Republican. Images of gleaming porcelain toilets and marble floors floated through my mind like a mirage.

Stephen asked me to participate in the mandala circle, which consisted of lying head to head with five other gullible souls on a bed of burrs and dirt. I was a good sport. But the rest of the afternoon was spent picking burrs off my ass. New spiritual heights were not reached, although my status seemed to rise in Stephen's eyes.

"It's so great sharing this with you," he said, " 'cause this is really like introducing you to my family."

These were not the in-laws I had dreamed about. Yet, as his desire for me grew, ("Want to go back to the tent and make love?") mine diminished, overcome by a more fervent desire to commune with a bathtub and my Sealy Posturepedic pillow-top mattress.

As I clutched my stomach and grimaced, Stephen introduced me to trapeze artists, fire-eaters, jugglers, puppeteers, clowns and a woman who used to live in a tree. They discussed goddess energies, the power of menstrual flow, shakra opening techniques, and the most efficient way to build a yurt. They compared gurus and brands of yoga, and then said things like, "At least we're not spiritually competitive."

At Kidlantis (the playground where hippies brought their spawn to learn their foreign ways) Stephen taught me how to make puppets out of recycled water bottles. Following this we visited the Casbah hemp tent to listen to tribal-earth-trance-dance music. We passed open-air massage stations where scantily clad bodies moaned in ecstasy. I tried to act unfazed by the naked toddlers dancing inside a metal cage beneath a peace sign. We made our way through the electronic music dome, stepping around hypnotically writhing dancers, bodies strewn across pillows, couples converging in psycho-spiritual communal trances as swirling multi-colored lights blinded us, music throbbed in our ears and the stench of marijuana filled our nostrils.

The evening drumming circle was led by Mickey Hart, some Grateful Dead rock star whom everyone had heard of but me. Just as I began to think it might be time to get some rest, Hart induced the masses to bang on their drums in a clamorous cacophony of sound. How this was intended to influence global politics I have yet to determine. Miniature hippie clones marched onto the stage to declare their desire for world peace, each child bearing a name more new-age than the last. First came Harmony, a blonde toddler who declared, "All I want is love." Next came Shanti, who lilted into the microphone, "Let the light in . . . [pregnant pause] Feel the light." Then came Sky, Shalom, Summer and Rain. I panicked, wondering if Stephen and I would have to mortify our future child with a name that could be confused for an eau-de-cologne.

At midnight I used my illness as an excuse to skip out on the all-night rave. The night was endless, icy and deafening.

Stephen returned to our tent rapturous, only to discover me swathed head to toe in sleeping bags, thermal underwear, three pairs of socks, scarf, gloves, and hat. My ears were plugged, my eyes covered by an eye-pillow and my nose tumescent and chafed, a pile of tissues accumulating in the corner like the leaning tower of Pisa. Needless to say, our tent did not rock on this night. It was sometime near dawn (while the final band was warming up) that I gave up hope of our relationship ever succeeding, due to irreconcilable differences.

As the sun rose, Stephen walked (I ran) to my once-silver car now camouflaged by a layer of dirt. Inside he helped me shed my clothes piece by piece. Upon the immaculate plush leather of my car seats, listening to the soothing melodies of Chopin he did things to me that reconverted me to his cause. The car rocked. And for a moment, I could have sworn we were on the French Riviera.

Waiting for the Other Wingtip to Drop

by Charles West

I DIDN'T KNOW IT AT THE TIME, but my bad luck began when the pilot aborted our take-off from San Francisco to avoid hitting a single-engine plane taxiing in front of us on a crossing runway.

It was the summer of 1983, a time of anxiety for me with the January 1, 1984, deadline for the break-up of the monolithic Ma Bell fast approaching. I was an analyst in Pacific Bell's pricing department and had been given a "career development opportunity" to lead a nation-wide task force on top of my regular assignments. I wasn't looking forward to my Denver trip, where I'd have to mask my superficial knowledge of the issues and bluff my way through another presentation.

Soon the plane was flying east. Our initial descent over the Rockies was turbulent. I relaxed as we flew over the airport and made our final approach. We circled for an hour before the pilot confirmed what many of us were thinking. There's a problem with our landing gear, he explained; Denver ground staff was preparing a secondary runway for our touchdown, just 15 minutes away. A flight attendant explained how to brace ourselves for an emergency landing, not that it made much difference to 6-foot 8-inch passengers like me who have no wiggle room in cramped economy seats.

The pilot's quarter-hour promise ballooned to an hour. The landing gear held. At the all-clear signal, I popped out of my seat, feeling like a cork that had just been pried from a wine bottle.

That morning, San Francisco had been enjoying a typical summer day—cool, foggy and comfortable. Now I crouched in the car rental shuttle, trying not to bonk my head on the ceiling. Lowering my head to exit I managed to catch my wingtip on a step and shear off the entire heel.

After ratcheting the rental car's air conditioning controls up to the max and forcing the seat all the way back, I changed into my running shoes. The end-of-rush-hour drive toward town was stop-and-go, and I recalled how bad things supposedly happened in threes. Twice was a coincidence, but three was a pattern. As an analyst, I was an expert on data patterns.

The multi-story hotel was easy to find in an upscale residential Denver neighborhood. Since it was after 6, I counted on dashing out early the next morning for a quick shoe repair prior to my 10 o'clock presentation. Remember this was back before casual Friday.

Check-in proceeded without incident. On the way to my room, I anticipated a quiet meal and then a successful search of the Yellow Pages for a nearby shoe shop.

When I entered my room I was startled to hear a woman shriek my name. Stowing black lingerie into her dresser was Ms. G, a Pacific Bell marketing manager. She was in Denver attending another marketing meeting. Something about the room's lighting or my looming presence made her upper lip perspire and highlighted her slight mustache. After eyeing me suspiciously, she seconded my gallant offer to find a different room for the night. In 1983 companies weren't as consumed with cost cutting as they are today, and we assumed we weren't meant to share a room to save expenses.

Back at the front desk, I approached the young red-haired woman who'd checked me in. Reluctantly she broke away from bantering co-workers to deal with me.

"Excuse me," I said, "there's been some mistake. My room is already occupied."

"Room number?" she said, chewing her gum with irritating snaps and crackles.

"It's 918. Anyway, the occupant is a woman."

"All part of our frequent guest reward package. Name?"

Eventually she upgraded me to a vacant top-floor suite. It had an impressive view of the mountains and a gigantic bed.

I had a pleasant dinner with a colleague, then found the ad of a cobbler who opened at 9 a.m. I reviewed my presentation while listening to a radio station with an eclectic play list, ranging from folksinger Sandy Denny to new age pianist George Winston. After organizing my notes and slides for the morning's grilling, I reflected on the day's spate of bad luck. Four unwelcome events. What were the odds I'd suffer two more tomorrow? Whom could I lobby for a reprieve? I wasn't asking the Fates to grant me anything too demanding: Just get my shoe repaired quickly and let my presentation be well-received. By noon I'd be one step closer to reducing this inappropriate assignment to another bullet point on my résumé.

At a quarter to 9 the next morning, feeling self-conscious in my pin-striped suit and running shoes, I carried a map and my damaged wingtip to the car, which I had no trouble locating; it was the one with a flat tire. The hotel's front desk staff arranged for a service station attendant to change the flat.

A chatty Greek cobbler restored my wingtip. By 9:50 a.m. I was back at the hotel exchanging pleasantries with task force members and potential interrogators. I didn't list to starboard as I approached the podium. And—was there any doubt?—my presentation dazzled the audience. I credit my strategy of starting off with a recap of my bad luck. This admission drew a few smiles from the normally dour economists and statisticians, who revel in first-hand accounts of others' misfortunes. By the time I got on with the morning's agenda, the audience seemed to be in a generous mood; no questions about translogarithmic indirect utility functions were lobbed my way.

Gazing out my window on the flight home, I thought of a song I'd heard that morning, John Denver's version of "Leaving on a Jet Plane." The line, "don't know when I'll be back again," made me think about the theory of threes. Denver is still shuffling its deck of cards, hoping to deal me one more joker off the bottom. An opportunity was lost when the plane took off without a hitch. Perhaps my assignment to the task force counted as my first stroke of bad luck, pushing my total to six, and either rescuing me from further trouble or setting me up for a new set of three. The only way to find out would be to confront Denver head on and gather more data, a scenario about as likely as the Bell System or Humpty Dumpty being put back together again.

Car Trouble

by Jean B. Hauser

IT WAS THE PERFECT CHRISTMAS PRESENT. No airline security, cramped coach seating or theme park mobs. All my husband and I had to do was drive from our Virginia home over the border to Tennessee and check into a beautiful Blue Ridge Mountains condo, courtesy of our son.

Just 25 miles from our Foothills Parkway destination the transmission failed. My husband backed our truck down a winding single lane road until we could safely pull over. A wrecker dropped us off at a dealer in Newport where, unfortunately, no rentals were available. The problem was solved by taking a taxi—only 45 miles to the friendly rental car office at our destination, Gatlinburg.

Early Sunday morning we returned to Newport and recovered the luggage left behind in the truck. A day later we doubled back to the Newport dealership to discuss our car with the mechanic. Returning to Gatlinburg we took a side trip to Pigeon Forge. Unfortunately our brakes locked up. Fortunately we were on a relatively flat road. Back at the Gatlinburg rental car office a replacement car was waiting. A day later we turned this vehicle in and rented another car in Newport, hoping that would simplify the process of picking up our repaired truck.

Back in Newport the mechanic had bad news—there was a major problem in the truck's year-old engine. Our car would not be available until the following Tuesday. Since we had to return home Sunday to be at work on Monday, the only solution was to rent a truck and car carrier in Knoxville.

Unfortunately, just as we were leaving to pick up the truck and car carrier, we learned that the Knoxville agency had rented the vehicle we'd reserved to another customer. Now it was old reliable U Haul in Greenville to the rescue. Unfortunately the U Haul reservation desk gave us terrible directions that led us 35 miles out of our way. We reached U Haul at noon, the same time the rental car was due. After completing the paperwork, we rushed back toward Newport hoping to return the car within the one-hour grace period. As I followed my husband out of the parking lot, I noticed that the truck's turn signals were reversed. Literally, the left signal did not know what the right signal was doing. An hour and a half later, after correcting this problem, we were on our way.

By the time we reached Newport, it was clear we weren't going to make the entire 450-mile journey home in a day. We decided to spend the night in Roanoke, a town flooded by heavy rainstorms. Saturday morning we drove over the Blue Ridge Mountains in thick fog and rain. Just 20 miles from home our vehicle was sideswiped by another truck. Our vehicle's big left side mirror, glass and frame smashed through the window. My husband received small cuts on his arm and a lot of scratches on his new glasses, but otherwise we were fine. After we dealt with the police—who attributed the accident to a pair of big trucks on a narrow road—we drove home with rain pouring in our smashed window.

How was the condo, you ask? There was a tornado

nearby, and tremendous hailstorms one evening. While I was reading at 2 a.m., the light blew. And we never did find a can opener. Otherwise it was a perfect vacation.

Cinque Terrible

by Shirley Lawyer

SOLO BACKPACKING IS A GOOD WAY TO SEE WESTERN EUROPE, particularly Cinque Terre, a string of five quaint towns on the northern Mediterranean. These towns are famous for their vibrantly colored buildings that grasp sheer rock cliffs and outcroppings on the ocean. A marvel of engineering and craftsmanship, these structures appear to be the work of a special effects department. Because of the difficult terrain, no roads connect these towns. Your only transportation options are train, boat and trail.

The southernmost town in Cinque Terre is Riomaggiore, home of a hostel named Mama Rosa's. The owner herself meets the trains daily to guide the world's youth to her noisy establishment that is heaven for felines. By this point in my journey I had already experienced heinous conditions in the hostels of seven other countries and developed a "bring it on" attitude. I looked forward to the challenge of finding cheap but tolerable lodgings in Cinque Terre.

When I stepped off the train in Riomaggiore, I felt an obligation to be one of those who survived a couple of nights at Mama Rosa's. At the hostel our group was greeted by her son, a chubby, hairy, dentally challenged man who reminded me of a Muppets character named Sweetums, right down to the snaggletooth. He mumbled incoherently as he checked us in, took our lire and showed us to our rooms.

I set out to explore the town on this very warm September day and ended up at the water's edge staring into an inviting little cove on the Mediterranean. Lacking a swimsuit, I wasn't about to miss a chance to enjoy one of the places you are supposed to see before you die. With not a soul in sight, I stripped down to bra and panties and jumped in the water for my first swim in the Italian Riviera. In less than five minutes, a man my age appeared from nowhere, followed by a friend. "Hey, how's it going? We're from California. Mind if we join you?"

As a matter of fact I did mind and I left. Afterward, I showered and went to find a restaurant. Very quickly I discovered that reservations were mandatory even at the tail end of high season. My dinner consisted of what I carried in my backpack: Nutella and crackers. Luckily, my friendly Canadian bunkmates had purchased several bottles of wine and helped me drink enough to forget my swimsuit fiasco.

The next day I decided to hike the eight-mile trail linking the five towns perfect for exploring, ride the train back to Riomaggiore and enjoy a nice, relaxed dinner at La Lanterna, the local hot spot for authentic Italian seafood dishes. My reservation was secure.

The following morning my legs were covered with flea bites, courtesy of Mama Rosa's cats. Itching aside, my agenda was solid. I made sure my one precious towel was hung out to dry, grabbed my daypack and set off.

Winding through ancient terraced olive groves and vineyards, the steep and rugged trail clings to the rocky coastline. By the time I reached Monterosso, the last of the five towns, I was hot, dusty, sweaty and looking forward to a refreshing swim before catching the train. Again I found a private cove, stripped down to bra and panties and dove in.

I was floating on my back when I heard voices at the end of a nearby jetty. There was company, a very tan, very nude blonde couple diving into the water. No problem. As long as they steer clear of my daypack, they were welcome to share my space. Their swim was over quickly. Soon they were sunning themselves on the rocks, far from my pack while I floated and meditated

Suddenly I heard a boat jetting toward me in the distance. I would have had plenty of time to get out of its path if the boat's captain had been watching the water instead of the naked woman sunning on the rocks. I swam desperately for shore, my head and arms flaying madly about, trying to make my naked self more visible. They never saw me and I just missed being decapitated by the disgusting skipper and his perverted crew. The boat's wake washed over the rock that held my daypack, shoes and clothes. I wrung out my belongings as best I could and spread them on boulders to dry. The train schedule forced me into those still damp clothes for the journey back to Riomaggiore. I walked back to the station and boarded the first train south.

I was hungry, tired and ready to forget about the headline that would have made page one in the Medford, Oregon, *Daily Mail*. "Local Woman Sliced and Diced by Peeping Toms." There was just enough time for a lukewarm shower before making my way to La Lanterna, where the promise of a delicious dinner with lots of excellent local wine warmed me. But as the train approached Riomaggiore I noticed it wasn't slowing down. We continued on to La Spezia, the next town on the line. I had to wait 25 minutes to catch the correct train back to Riomaggiore.

Back at Mama Rosa's I discovered a cat sleeping on my

pillow, my backpack shoved crudely under my bunk amid mounds of dust bunnies and cat hair and my only towel stolen. By now the saltwater in my clothes combined with the flea bites on my legs were making me itch. Who had stolen my towel? Maybe it was those Canadians. I searched everywhere, but it was hopeless. Afraid my clothes would be next, I refused to leave them out to dry and marched my itchy, salty self to La Lanterna, where the vino was excellent. The next day I left for Rome via train, where my emergency-only credit card bought me one night in a clean, flea- and cat-free room with private shower and plush towels.

Sublet This

by Eugene Wildman

FOR MORE THAN A YEAR I had planned my trip to Thailand, a part of the world that I loved but had not been back to for nearly two decades. Once I took it for granted that was where I would live, only things had not worked out that way. All that remained was to sublet my apartment.

I was not out to clear a profit but merely cut my losses. It would be a cinch, I thought. I placed ads, but two weeks passed with no response. I registered with the off-campus housing offices at area universities and medical schools and went back to waiting.

Somebody would be getting a steal, after all. Four months in a Chicago apartment, utilities included, for $500. Could you beat it? As departure time drew closer my optimism began to give way. I was going on borrowed money as it was. But to swallow a four-month rent bite, too?

With a week and a half to go, I finally got a break. A friend of a friend knew a third party who would be in Chicago for the time I would be gone. This person was a performance artist who was taking part in a series of workshops connected with the peace movement. Great. I was for peace, too. No intervention in Central America. End imperialism. End apartheid. I hired a cleaning woman to get the place spotless, left keys and a bank deposit slip with my friend, and went off to Asia with a happy heart.

I should have known better. When I got back, about a week early, I took a cab home. I took it for granted there would be no objections if I simply dropped my bags off. I rang the downstairs bell but there was no answer. Wearily, I let myself into the lobby, but the apartment was chain-locked from inside. I left my bags outside the door and trudged downstairs and around the back way. The back door opened easily enough, but when I gripped the door-knob it came off in my hands.

That was only a prelude. Nothing could have prepared me for what was inside. Every piece of furniture had been moved. Every single stick. What had been the living room was now the bedroom. What was the bedroom had become the living room. Even the stove and refrigerator were moved. Not far, but they were moved. The painting that previously had hung in the living room was now above the kitchen sink. A Japanese print that was above my desk had been folded. Smudge marks ran down the sides. Another, of Edvard Munch's The Shriek, had disappeared altogether. In the bathroom were two shlock five and dime landscapes.

It turns out my sublet had not paid a dime of rent while availing himself of the free utilities and record collection and books. He even went away for a week and let someone else use the place. Records were loaned out, and a lovely piece of luggage was filched that had been given to me as a present. In its place was a pressed cardboard monstrosity he had apparently arrived with. I walked through the apartment for days afterward, thinking: "This is the performance, this is art."

My Purple Heart

by Nadine Michele Payn

AT 2:30 IN THE MORNING the clock radio jolted me awake. I willed myself out of bed and careened into the bathroom to splash cold water on my face. "Why do I torture myself like this?" I muttered to the mirror. Actually I do it every year for my family's summer vacation. Belize is only a 3½-hour journey from our house as the crow flies, but jetliners have obligations.

Our 6 a.m. San Francisco flight heads for Houston, where we catch a connection to Belize City. After customs and immigration we hop on a puddle-jumper to Ambergris Caye, a coral atoll on the strand of islands that form the longest barrier reef in the Western Hemisphere. We arrive at dusk, grimy and exhausted. But the turquoise Caribbean glistening in morning's light always rewards our perseverance.

That's what kept me going on this dark Berkeley night as I quickly dressed and waited for the airport shuttle. Our bags were lined up at the front door with my comatose daughter slumped against them. My husband, who was winding up a summer school course, would join us a week later. The hall clock ticked as 3 a.m. came and went. Anxiously I phoned the shuttle dispatcher at 3:16.

"Yeah, the driver's on his way, don't worry," he said.

"Maybe he's lost," I suggested. "It's hard to find our house at night. Can you try to reach him?"

Silence, then finally the dispatcher's voice, "Sorry, I can't raise him—our cell phones don't work too good in the hills. But I know he's on his way, so don't worry, he should be there any minute."

Five more minutes ticked by. I called back. Same dispatcher. Same story. I grabbed the Yellow Pages and called a taxi company. No answer. Then another. Yes, they could get a cab to me in maybe 45 minutes. I said I'd call back and hung up. I debated waking up my husband but remembered that when he'd come home, exhausted from long hours of teaching, he'd had a couple of glasses of wine. Between the alcohol and his fatigue, he was an unlikely candidate for chauffeur. I called for the cab.

It was 3:41 on my digital watch. Our instructions were to check in at San Francisco International by 4 a.m. Still hoping the shuttle driver would make a miraculous appearance sooner than the taxi, I walked outside and searched the darkness. Nobody in sight.

By now I was certain we would miss our flight. Even if it were possible to book another within the next few days, I'd lose money on these tickets and would have to pay full fare for new ones. I studied my watch again with the intensity of a microbiologist looking at a lab slide.

Fourteen minutes later a couple of loud raps rattled the front door. Through the peephole I saw a tall man with a pudgy baby face and a blonde ponytail. Large biceps protruded from the sleeves of a white T-shirt. A tattooed dragon decorated one arm.

"Hey, you can open the door lady. I'm Jack from the airport shuttle."

"Where the heck have you been?" I yelled, unlocking the door.

"Where have you been, lady?" he answered. "I've been waiting for you up at the street level!"

I knew he was lying. My instincts flashed a warning. This guy's energy was not good. On the other hand, just because he was a brat didn't mean he was dangerous.

"C'mon Mom, let's go, let's just GO!" came a voice.

My daughter had sprung to life and was out the door, rolling her eyes along with her carry-on. I quickly canceled the cab and followed her. Once inside the van, making good time on the nearly empty freeway, I felt a little calmer. But I let Jack know my opinion about his attitude. He remained remorseless.

We pulled into SFO at 4:46 a.m. and went to the back of the van to get our luggage. It was still dark, with few travelers in sight. Reaching for my wallet, I wondered how much money to give Jack. His contemptuous behavior ruled out a tip and a discount off the $50 fare was not unreasonable. I pulled out a $20 and a $10 and handed them over.

"You owe me $20 more," Jack demanded.

"Sorry, Jack," I retorted. "We didn't get full-fare service. I deserve a discount for the stress you caused. Believe me, I would rather pay $50 and not have gone through such aggravation." My daughter and I began dragging the luggage to the curb.

"Lady, I'm not budging till you give me another 20 bucks!"

"Mom," pleaded my daughter, "just give him the money and go."

"Sweetie, he doesn't deserve it. It's the principle of the thing."

I turned to Jack and looked him in the eyes.

"I'm not giving you any more money. You're lucky to be getting what you're getting!"

Jack's face reddened.

"Then you can kiss your luggage good-bye," he snarled.

He snatched our bags off the curb, threw them back into the van and was about to slam the hatch shut.

"Oh no you don't," I screamed and grabbed the handle of one valise. Jack blocked my move, I parried, he shoved, I pushed back. My daughter froze.

"Ana, help me! Don't just stand there!"

She didn't budge. "Mom, please, give him the money and go."

I couldn't go. I was desperate to win the fight. I had to get our luggage. Besides our tropical clothing, it contained our snorkel/dive gear, carefully chosen novels and special gifts for our Belizean friends.

My right hand found a valise handle, and I tugged on it with all my strength. Jack escalated and twisted my arm hard. It hurt like hell, but I didn't let go of that handle. Meanwhile, my rational mind knew the scene was surreal. My ferocious combat was happening in the midst of routine airport business: Cars were pulling over nearby to discharge passengers who waved cheerful good-byes. No one noticed me.

I screamed for help. Two uniformed female security guards stood near the terminal entrance only a few yards away. They gave me desultory looks and turned their heads. With an adrenalin surge that shocked me, I pulled my valise out of the van. Jack locked onto my wrist, immobilizing me. Quickly I lowered my head as if I was going to bite his hand.

"Jesus Christ, lady. What, are you crazy? What the f——
are you doing, trying to bite me!"

He released his hold. In that instant, I seized the other
large bag and commanded the still frozen Ana to thaw and
grab the two carry-ons. We raced inside the terminal to the
ticket counter.

I stood panting. Ana was angry.

"Mom, you're crazy! I can't believe you didn't just give
that jerk the money. You were a wild woman!"

I was trembling too much to respond. After a few minutes of calming myself, I heard Ana yelp, "Mom, Jack's
inside the terminal. He's talking to a policewoman!"

Sure enough, they were coming toward me. Heads
turned as the cop pulled me off the line. Flushed with fear
and embarrassment, I asked Ana to save our place. Jack
had stepped back a few paces but was watching me and
gloating.

I told my side of the story and said if I was able to call
the dispatcher he'd verify my version of events, certainly
that Jack had arrived at my house seriously late. The policewoman escorted me to a pay phone. I got the dispatcher
on the line, he listened and put his manager on the phone.
That fellow heard me, then said, "I'm sorry you feel that
way, but you really do owe us the $20."

He added I could write to the company and complain,
but there was no way around the fact that I needed to give
Jack the money. Finally I hung up.

"I can take you to the police station, and you can press
charges for battery," the policewoman offered. I felt vin-
dicated and briefly considered the idea, but going to the
station would insure we'd miss the flight to Belize City.

"I did the best I could," I replied. "But I want to be on

the plane, and my daughter wants to be on that plane, so I'll have to give the guy his 20 bucks."

She gave a noncommittal nod and chaperoned me the short distance to where Jack was standing with a smirk wider than the wingspan of a 767. I handed over the cash and didn't say a word. Neither did he.

I thanked the policewoman as Jack lumbered away and got back in line. At last we reached the counter. Suddenly Ana screamed. What now?

"Mom, Jack dropped your $20. Look, it's over there near the other ticket counter!"

Sure enough, there it was on the floor. I looked up and saw Jack nearing the glass exit doors. I knew what I had to do.

I told Ana to stay at the counter and raced towards the bill, certain that at any second Jack would realize he had dropped it. I bent down and grabbed the greenback. Relishing my triumph, my better nature made an appearance. Wouldn't it be a moral victory, a greater feat, to give the money back?

As Jack headed out the doors, I ran over and tapped his shoulder. Putting on my best Buddha smile, I intoned,

"Jack, I believe you're missing something important!"

He spun around, and I handed him the $20 with a flourish. He looked amazed, "blown away," Ana would say later. He mumbled something that sounded like thanks and shuffled into the pre-dawn darkness.

I'm pleased to tell you the rest of our journey to Belize was wonderfully uneventful. The next morning we woke up to a brilliant sun and the soft sound of the tradewinds rustling through palm fronds. The water was its usual perfect turquoise, and the reef was a thin white line where sea meets sky. As I put on my bathing suit, I noticed my right arm ached. Had I slept on it badly? I walked out on the verandah for a better look. There on my forearm was a raised purple bruise the size of a plum. Jack's signature.

I contemplated my injury, then turned to Ana.

"Sweetie," I said proudly, "please take a photo of my battle wound. It's my purple heart."

She dutifully snapped the shot which, framed in silver, now hangs on my bedroom wall alongside a drawing she made of a $20 bill nestled peacefully in the palms of a Buddha of Compassion.

Under a Honey Moon on Kauai

by Bryan Vincent Knapp

WE PLANNED A SIMPLE AND STANDARD HONEYMOON to Kauai, following the footsteps of Mark Twain, Jack London and my parents. The utter lack of originality even made me comfortable and self-assured. Were we venturing to Bali or Annapurna, following a branch of the Silk Road, or renting a Land Rover and making our careful, sandy way to Timbuktu, then I would be on the lookout for the wayside robber or the gasoline fire or the scorpion in my boot. As it was, we were remaining in America, just a jaunt to another state.

We landed on Kauai, located our rental car and easily drove the twisting roads and one-lane bridges of the northern edge of the island. We slept through the night and woke to a fine double rainbow bending and clarifying itself over the verdant mountains. And so we were married and the happiest newlyweds on the island. Our only timepiece was the vicissitudes of the tides and the rolling aim of the sun. We filled our days with adventure and excitement, hiking to 400-foot Hanakapiai Falls and swimming in the ensuing cold pool, allowing the water that felt like hail to fall on our shoulders. The guidebooks all warn about swimming in this pool for fear of falling rocks; no rocks fell that day. The guidebooks warn of sharks and scorpions and dangerous tides; our ocean swimming was easy and fresh.

The only considerations while snorkeling were whether we should term the water aquamarine or turquoise, the technicolor school of fish numbered 200 or 300, and were we too close to the sea turtles for their own comfort. A blissful ease followed us like the rays of the sun and the kiss of the continual trade winds.

Our confidence acute a week into our journey, we decided to brave what *National Geographic* calls the second-best adventure in North America: a kayak trip of the forbidding and remote Na Pali coast. No roads meet this coast, and only one hiking trail graces the precipitous mountains. This is a 17-mile journey that may be broken into casual segments or blasted in one day. Our guided tour was of the one-day variety.

We wore long-sleeve shirts and wore plenty of sunscreen, hats were obligatory, and we brought enough water and easy snacks. My newly minted wife, Silby, and I shoved off with our kayak mates and began plying the tossing ocean water with our paddles. We did achieve the necessary exclamations of a tourist's ecstasy in the water under those towering, vertical cliffs. We oohed and ahhed righteously when the sea turtle breached and breathed, and felt a natural awe upon entering darkened sea caves, dipping around a careful Hawaiian monk seal in one and paddling underneath a waterfall in another. After a while, my wrist began to throb. I ignored it; a tough guy paddling with the best of them. I was in the rear of our kayak, and the pedal rudder stopped working. I had to steer with the paddle, in tricky cave terrain and in increasingly choppy water.

Waves eager for landfall find none on this stretch of Kauai; there is no beach, and the perpendicular cliffs fall into the water straight. The waves hit them and bounce backward, creating an unavoidable froth that tosses a yellow fiberglass craft. We held our paddles perhaps too rigidly, fighting to remain upright during severe water. A dad and his son from Kansas City fell in the drink. The kid in the kayak floated away at two knots while the dad bobbed behind, a lone speck in the huge expanse. Dad had to be rescued by Ivan the Guide.

At this point, with Kansas City Dad rescued and then spilled again, each vigorous and nervous paddle shot strokes of agony up my arm. I was 10 miles along this wild and wicked stretch of coast and there was no place to land, and I'd be damned if I was going to be the one helicoptered or catamaraned by the authorities out of there. Nope, to grin and bear was my fate.

Silby squelched a scream because we were not alone. She lurched backward and held her foot, struggling with what looked like fishing line. "Damn, she's hooked and bleeding," I thought. But I thought wrong. Silby's lip was quivering, and I knew that were we alone this trip would be over, the rescue helicopters welcomed, and she would allow the bawling to unabashedly commence. But Silby the Trouper, Silby the Brave, bit her lip and held back the tears, with some effort.

"Po-Jo!" shouted Melissa, the other guide, to Ivan, who turned back to see if we were okay. Portuguese Man-o-Wars are related to jellyfish, and they bear a vicious sting when you touch their very thin and trailing tentacles. They do not swim as other jellyfish do but cruise in multitudes on the surface, then easily ride a splash into your little boat. "It's like being stung by 50 bees at once," said Silby. Our guidebook, we discovered later, described it as 1,000.

Kansas City Son asked Melissa while she was attending Silby, "Can I take a pee break now?" To take a pee break you jump in the water and hold on to the kayak's line. "No!" shouted Melissa, "This is not a good spot." When her attention was turned back to my wife, K.C. Son jumped anyway. He was immediately stung by a Po-Jo. He screamed and clambered gracelessly back into his boat, nearly toppling his dad into the drink for a third time. Ivan dealt with his sting. A woman next to us shouted out and grabbed her arm. I began to duck for cover. I rolled down my long sleeves, covered my sunburned legs in a towel and pulled down my hat. This is war, Mr. Portuguese, come get me if you can.

I paddled through the pain in my wrist for the remainder of the 17 miles, attempting to smile heartily when Ivan had us observe yet another natural phenomenon, another steep cliff or waterfall, another romantic isolated beach. We were thankful to reach our destination, weary and spent and stung. We felt like proud expeditioners, argonauts and questateers, no whining about a blister here or there. We ate well and drank well and ultimately slept well that night, pleased with ourselves and our grand honeymoon.

The next week ensued without a glitch or pestering hitch. We moved from our rented condo and left the car at exotic beaches and trailheads. I couldn't do anything with my right hand, but that's beside the point. And Silby's Po-Jo ridges and bumps were merely the scars for future storytelling. We decided to camp our last three nights on the beach in our tent.

The first evening was calm and joyous, easy under a palm and on a sandy bluff. We swam at dusk and at dawn. This was at Ha'ena County Park, near the trailhead of the Kalalau Trail and the beginning of the Na Pali cliffs. Waving foliage and skying mountains give weight to any poet who employs "shark tooth" to describe a peak.

We left the north and drove to the south, proudly avoiding the resorts of Poi'pu, and down to Salt Pond Park Campground. Here the winds arriving from the northeast were trading in a brutal swiftness. All the sites with bush buffers and stone protection were taken. We struggled to find a spot. Finally, and quite bravely, we picked a place on a bluff, directly in the driving wind, claiming that we would weigh the thing down with our gear, stake it profoundly, and all would be well. Our bodies provided the weight on the first night. We slept well and swam in the morning before the lifeguard arrived at his orange survival lookout stand with his longboard.

Tourists or European travelers or hippies fond of hostels did not habituate Salt Pond. Rather, it was the party zone of a band of hardcore locals. I won't delve into how loud they were or how late they stayed awake into the night; or the sound system they employed as a party tool, hiphop and reggae till 1 a.m. at disco decibels; or the preternatural screeching of 15 small children whose only role appeared to be to run about pell-mell and sleep not one wink. All spoke in the native island tongue. They stared at us curiously.

We stayed out late that day, watched the sunset at Spouting Horn, an inspiring jut of black volcanic rock hollowed by centuries of pounding Hawaiian no-joke surf. A tunnel has been created by waves, and a release valve inland by 20 feet. The waves arrive, marching one after the other, and they enter the hole and shoot out the release valve 30 feet into the air, accompanied by a loud belch and groan from within the earth. It compares well with any other landmark spout or geyser, including Old Faithful. It was here that we gazed upon the sunset, as honeymoon romantics, of course, and where we watched the golden, honey-colored moon rise. Filled with the sagacity of spirit that arrives upon the calm, we went out to eat at a local joint and then drove south for our campground.

Earlier we'd made a pact, complete with a handshake and a clink of our new wedding bands. This oath was serious stuff, and I aimed to see it through. I detected, however, that Silby was waffling. Our admonitions of seriousness were to take a night swim, under the waxing honey moon as it sat aloft above the ocean, its light cast the way human beings love it on the shimmering water. "We might as well not be married if we can't do this," I said. The wind was howling as we walked toward our campsite.

As I was attempting to remind Silby of our oath and to talk her into swimming on this night, I kept looking ahead to our camping bluff. No tent. I dared not share this with Silby, who is occasionally known to panic and call out the National Guard. We were closer to our bald, empty space. Hopeful always, I still held to my reserves.

"There they are!" shouted one of our neighbors, a native woman. All 12 heads in their compound, under a pavilion, music blaring, turned toward us. "Your tent flew in the ocean!" the woman's son exclaimed. I thought his tone a bit too gleeful, given the circumstances.

"What?" Silby said without hesitation. The worst was already assumed.

"The wind blew your tent into the ocean," the teenage boy repeated. "And we saved it!" He added the last bit in a shout. "The lifeguard jumped from his stand and ran in. I jumped in the water too, and we both dragged it out. It's over there, under the picnic table."

Sure enough, our wet, collapsed and bundled tent was jammed underneath the picnic table. We dragged it out, with the neighborhood children gathering to observe the show. The wind was still blowing hard and steady, making it difficult to set up a tent. The glowing moon cast its gentle light on the water.

We set up the tent and unzipped the sides, finding two sopping fleece jackets and sad down sleeping bags. "Let's take everything out and tie it to the tent frame," Silby said. "The wind will dry it out in 30 minutes. In the meantime, let's do our moonlight swim." I looked at her, surprised.

The children dissipated back to their games, and we stripped to the skin. We peered at the glowing, honey moon, and dove into the dark, warm water. We swam and laughed and kissed twice in that strip where moonlight and sea embrace. The wind, meanwhile, worked on our soaked gear, and my mind cast aside thoughts about silent warship jellyfish sailing the salty sea around us.

The No-Star Cruise

by Richard Menzies

"IT'S LOVELY ON A RAFT!" said Huckleberry Finn as he and Jim drifted lazily down America's mainstream. Finn was fortunate that his big river adventure was plotted by Mark Twain, an experienced river pilot, and not by the Green River Marathon Association.

The event was called the Memorial Day Friendship Cruise. Along with 500 other privately owned motorboats we intended to cruise downstream from Green River, Utah, on the Mighty Green to its confluence with the Colorado, then upstream to Moab. Total distance, 182 miles, most of it through rugged canyon country devoid of human settlement and with only two exit points: Mineral Wells and Anderson Bottom. Boaters who ran into trouble anywhere else along the route would be on their own.

I had been invited along as a reporter by local boosters eager for publicity. Newly married, I brought along my wife, Anne, for an inexpensive "cruise" honeymoon. For the first time, the event had attracted two celebrities—Jana Cegavski and Pat Klipper, who paired on television's *Dating Game*. This was their dream date. Even though it was an unseasonably cold and blustery day in May, the two managed wan smiles as we were introduced. Jana looked a lot like the actress Karen Allen, while Pat reminded me of Bob Denver in *Gilligan's Island*. Their designated skipper was a dead ringer for Alan Hale, Jr.

As Jana, Pat and their chaperone were fitted with life-jackets, I prepared to record the event for posterity. In these pre-video camcorder days, I was shooting a 16mm film camera manufactured by Bell & Howell. The DR-70 was driven by an internal main-spring wound by cranking a key much like an alarm clock or a wind-up toy. However, the DR-70 was not a toy. Folklore had it that fully half the combat cameramen who perished during World War II were felled by Bell & Howell mainsprings. When the thing snapped, an operator bracing the camera against his forehead at the time was in grave danger. His brain would bang against his skull like the clapper of Burma's great Mingum Bell.

By the time we arrived at the river, most of the flotilla had already left. Our escort, Marv Summerville, cast off and soon his outboard engine sputtered and died. We ran aground less than a half-mile from the starting point—only 181 miles to go. Marv corrected the problem, a disconnected throttle link, and soon we were on our way.

As we headed downriver, Anne and I gratefully dug into the box lunch that had been prepared for us by the Green River Marathon Association. I had taken exactly one bite of my bologna sandwich when the outboard engine went into cardiac arrest. We paddled to the steep bank, where Anne and I clutched at overhanging willow branches, holding the craft steady against the current while Marv and Paul fiddled with the motor. "The throttle lever this time," Marv announced. Also a jammed transmission.

Paul volunteered to act as manual gear shifter, while Marv nursed the fragile throttle lever and linkage. For the next hour or so we chugged bravely along, scraping against sandbars, bumping over floating logs and crashing into the

occasional bloated cow. There were an amazing number of
dead cows in the river. Where were they all coming from?
I speculated there might be a Wyoming rancher upstream
who saved on freight by floating his livestock to the packing plant like so many pine logs. I put away my bologna
sandwich.

The engine developed a new noise. Again, Marv climbed
overboard to have a look, reporting that the dodgy gearbox
was kaput. Reluctantly, our skipper decided it was time to
hoist the yellow flag. Finally another boat came along. It
was occupied by a genial ophthalmologist named John and
his equally cheerful niece, Cheryl. "Uncle John" offered to
tow us to the nearest put out point at Mineral Bottom. It
turned out to be a long, hard haul—we ran aground re-
peatedly, broke two tow ropes and lost one paddle.

By the time we reached Mineral Wells, darkness was
nearly upon us. We put ashore just long enough to refuel
John's boat and bid a hasty farewell to Paul, Marv and
their African Queen. With some reservations, Anne and
I decided to press onward. After all, I was still on assignment and optimistic that eventually we might be able to
catch up with the dating game couple. Plus, we had a free
steak dinner waiting for us at Anderson Bottom.

Anderson Bottom. Brigadoon. Erewon. There are places that exist only in the minds of fantasy writers and sun-
stroked prospectors, and I'm convinced that Anderson
Bottom is surely one of them. Never did we catch sight of
a campfire, nor did we catch a whiff of sizzling T-bones.
Indeed, the only bones we encountered were the ones that
went bump in the night, as Uncle John failed to steer clear
of still another cowberg.

We decided at last to put ashore on a nameless beach

where we built a campfire and roasted our wet socks instead of marshmallows for s'mores. At dawn, we climbed out of our sleeping bags and set off in hot pursuit of the friendship flotilla and our elusive dating game couple. John's outboard was roaring and John himself was celebrating in high spirits, having downed half a bottle of Yukon Jack for breakfast. Soon we were skipping like a stone over sandbars, logs and cattle-logs. Our route was framed by towering sandstone cliffs amplifying the voice of our skipper who sounded like a Wicked Witch of the North in surround sound. While Cheryl rummaged through the cooler for additional jet fuel for John, Anne and I cowered in the stern, wondering why we had forgotten to bring along lifejackets.

At the confluence of the Green and the Colorado, John hung a sharp left, and our craft sputtered up a rapid called The Chute. I caught a fleeting glimpse of a sign that seemed to be suggesting a 180-degree turn: DANGEROUS RAPIDS AHEAD. DO NOT ENTER. We had just passed by the entrance to the dreaded Cataract Canyon. I thanked my lucky stars that we were headed in the opposite direction, upstream toward Moab.

We began overtaking other boats, and Uncle John splashed their passengers as we passed. Coarse epithets and rude hand gestures were exchanged. Anne and I tried to indicate by body language that we weren't actually members of the crew but merely embarrassed passengers. As John sprayed, we both prayed for Moab and Deliverance.

Suddenly the motor quit. Out of gas. Helpless, we drifted downstream toward the mouth of Cataract Canyon. So this is how it ends, I thought. Ours will be the first-ever assault by a drunk ophthalmologist upon the fearsome rapids of Cataract Canyon. Soon we will sleep with the catfish—or bob with the bloated cattle.

Our only hope was that someone we had recently splashed and alienated would come to our rescue, which is asking a lot, even on a so-called Friendship Cruise, kind of like the crew of a disabled U-boat begging a Liberty Ship for assistance. Finally, just as our little craft was about to be sucked into the maw of the River of No Return, help arrived in the form of an official Green River Marathon rescue boat bearing precious jerry cans of spare gasoline.

The remainder of the trip, I'm happy to report, was uneventful. Our skipper, apparently humbled by his brush with disaster, backed off the booze and the throttle. The clouds parted, the sun came out and for the first time we were able to sit back and enjoy the magnificent red rock scenery.

We arrived in Moab just as the local Lions Club was stowing the banquet tables and striking the "Welcome to Moab" banner. Boats had all been loaded onto trailers, the crowd had dissipated and barbecue pits were being doused. The dating game couple? I have no idea what became of them, but I'm hoping they survived.

Anne and I are still together, although for some reason she has never again accompanied me on another river trip. I've gone on to float Flaming Gorge and Westwater and shoot the rapids of both Desolation and Cataract canyons. I've come to agree with Huckleberry Finn that life on a raft is indeed lovely. The key is to take it easy, go with the flow and leave your outboard motor at home.

Marvelous Merv and the Beaver Boot Bunch

by Fern Burch

LOOKING AT OUR TUOLUMNE RIVER RAFTING PARTY outfitted from head to toe in our neoprene wetsuits, perfect for an El Nino year, you would have never known a Maginot Line went down the middle of our raft, dividing the Northern Californians from the Southern Californians. Two nation states under the same flag, we tried to find common ground in the Sierra. It wasn't easy.

The culture clash altered our experience in several ways. The "Angeleno" women pulled tiny mirrors and mascara out from under their wetsuits and began reapplying their eye makeup in the pouring rain. One of them was wearing sodden beaver boots over her wetsuit booties. The Angelenos also tried to smoke on their raft. Their uncomplaining guide merely positioned the raft so that the rapids would hit the Angelenos in the face each time they tried to light up a cigarette.

After returning home from this cross-cultural experience, I was surprised when my husband suggested another rafting trip on the Lower Kern, a Southern California river. This time Northern California friends would not be joining us to provide a protective shield of rationality. It would just be the Angelenos and us.

I eagerly agreed to the trip, my husband called the out-

93

fitter, and off we went. The peaceful evening drive down to the Kern was magical. We saw a snowy owl fly silently over our heads as we traversed the back roads down to the river.

Our whitewater companions turned out to be defense industry contractors who spent their days happily designing missile systems. They were not squeamish about the fact that their handiwork might annihilate the universe. They believed their work was contributing to "deterrence." And they insisted on rafting together. Among those who decided to throw his lot in with the MX Missile guys was Marvelous Merv, a World Wrestling Federation wrestler. Merv's dashing wardrobe included a cotton sweatshirt, cotton sweatpants, gold chains around his neck and right wrist and a big, heavy gold ring on his finger. Because Merv and the defense industry contractors rafted together, my husband and I shared the remaining raft with another couple and their teenage daughter.

There were no rapids on the Lower Kern River. Our small group, evenly divided between women and men, knew the meaning of teamwork, a real asset on a whitewater river where the ability of the paddlers to coordinate their strokes can turn a group of beginners into an effective crew. Our guide was so impressed that he decided to stage a rescue drill. He intentionally pulled our raft into a little riffle of water behind a tiny rapid, where the river's hydraulics would cause the boat to be stuck if we didn't paddle out. Another guide, alone in a third raft with our tents and our dinner, threw a line to pull us out of the river in case of a dangerous situation.

Unfortunately, the rope caught on my lifejacket snap, and instead of repositioning our boat, began to yank me out of the raft. My quick-thinking husband unsnapped the rope from the closure on my life jacket. Disaster averted, we paddled out of the rapid that had presented no danger until the guides tried to rescue us.

At our evening campfire, the defense contractors reveled in their patriotism. They were sure that the missile systems they were creating would be an effective bargaining chip President Reagan could use to keep the world safe for third-rate actors.

In a moment of silence, Marvelous Merv stepped forward for a brief soliloquy. "I'm 40 years old," he stated, "but it's okay." He paused for effect. "Because," he went on, "I have a 24-year-old girlfriend and we spend Saturday mornings together in bed watching *Leave it To Beaver.*

The following morning we were ready to take on "pinball," a medium-size Kern River rapid at the bottom of our run. It consisted of five rocks that were arranged like a giant slalom course. Pinball, with fairly consistent wave action and moderate drops, was an easy run for experienced rafters. Pinball would have been a breeze were it not for the fact that Marvelous Merv fell out of his boat during a traverse.

Merv popped up right next to my seat in the raft. Although he weighed at least 50 pounds more than I did, I grabbed his life jacket, and using all of my body weight, pulled him into my seat while I fell into the center of our raft. Zombielike, Merv didn't move or speak.

Only halfway through Pinball, the guide needed me to return to my seat and paddle, so I stood up and threw the big guy into the middle of the raft.

After we finished navigating the rapids, Merv finally spoke. "I lost my gold ring, but it's okay." Again Merv

paused for effect. "Because," he continued, "I'm insured."
That was all Merv had to say.

Today, somewhere, this guy walks, talks and watches
Leave It to Beaver because I pulled him out of the water.

The Gourd

by Susan Parker

PEOPLE BRING HOME ALL SORTS OF SOUVENIRS from Mexico.
Me? I brought home a gourd, a big one.

But this oversize vegetable was a piece of art. I got reli-
gion when I saw it.

I was in a tiny village, tucked against the purple Sierra
Madre of Sonora. I'd driven down a bumpy road, to a decaying church. Outside the chapel, high on a crumbling
adobe wall, a cactus was growing. Someone had seen Jesus
hovering around the thorny plant. For decades pilgrims
had worshipped it, leaving candles and throwing away
their crutches.

It was nearby this holy cactus that I first saw the
gourd.

Word of the amazing cactus leaked into guidebooks
and onto the Internet. Local women sold their handiwork
to the intrepid tourists who ventured down the road. As I
pulled my rented Subaru into the village square, a cloud of
dust swirled around me. Nearby was the rotting church, a
crafts shop, ancient bodega and fancy restaurant operated
by gringos who had moved south from Arizona to estab-
lish an overpriced gourmet dining experience patronized
by the Cessna set.

I slammed the car door shut and upset the tranquility of
the village. Dogs barked. Roosters crowed. Children came

out of nowhere. The ladies of the crafts co-op gathered at the front of their shop and fanned themselves. I headed straight for the gringo restaurant. I was thirsty.

"A margarita," I demanded. "That was a lonely road."

I sat down beside a couple from Montana and chatted with them as I drank one margarita and then another. I excused myself and stumbled toward the crafts shop. It was then that I saw the gourd. It was bigger than a basketball and lighter than a feather.

"I must have it," I shouted. "It is the most beautiful gourd in the world! Who grew this extraordinary vegetable?"

A wrinkled, toothless woman smiled. She pointed silently to herself.

"She is the grower," someone nearby said in English.

"How much?" I asked.

"Seven dollars," the grower answered quickly. I bought it and lurched back to the restaurant.

"My God, you bought my gourd," screeched the Montana woman with the facelift.

"Isn't it fabulous?"

"I'll sell it to you for $10," I replied.

"Oh honey," she answered in a raspy voice and took a long drag off her cigarette. "My husband has such a small jet, it will never fit inside. It's just a little Cessna."

"That's too bad," I answered. "I'm taking the bus back to the States and there is plenty of room. I'll put this gourd in the overhead compartment.

The blonde lady stared at me. Her smile was strained.

But the next evening, on the bus to Nogales, the gourd didn't fit in the overhead compartment or on the floor in front of my seat. I had to keep it on my lap for 10 hours.

At the border I carried the gourd into the U.S. and put it and myself on a Tucson-bound bus. After a two-hour ride I squeezed into a taxi and then into a crowded plane, all the time holding the gourd pressed against my chest.

The gourd did not fit in my house. It was too big. I gave it to my friend Craig. He placed the gourd on a pedestal in front of his bay view windows. At sunset now you can look out and see fog rolling across the water. The Bay Bridge twinkles. Rose light reflects off my gourd from its prominent place in the living room. It glows with a heavenly warmth that reminds me not to buy oversize trinkets when I am traveling in foreign places.

A Night at the Rainbow

by Jim Krois

THE STREETS OF PESHAWAR WERE DIRTY AND CROWDED and the heat inescapable. Every movement produced rivers of sweat. It was 1977, and I had just arrived on the Indus plain from Afghanistan. The bus ride via the Kyber Pass to this northwestern Pakistani town was finally over. Visions of a cool shower at the end of the trail lightened my steps as I walked down the congested main street toward the bazaars and a tourist hotel that I had heard about in Kabul.

In the amalgam of cultures flooding the bazaars of Peshawar, I could recognize Moslems, Hindus, Buddhists and Animists, all dressed in their local costumes and colors. The tribal peoples were identifiable by clans according to the color of their turbans: rust, black, white, brown, green. Local Pakistanis wore modern polyester white shirts and traditional baggy white cotton pants, pegged at the ankle. Women dressed in a variety of costumes, from the very elaborate headdresses adorned with bright silk and delicate silver chains and bangles, to a simple scarf with only a few gold threads. Some were covered head-to-foot in billowing *chardi* while others draped themselves in the 15-foot-long traditional sari. The neighborhood smelled of sweet incense, pungent curry and noxious excrement.

The alleys and side streets were dramatic. Small shops, not much bigger than a walk-in closet, lined these meandering lanes, selling everything and anything. Beautiful handmade carpets from Nuristan to the north were being sold next to hand-treadle sewing machines from Bangladesh. A tailor displaying his hand-fashioned garments of the latest styles was selling next to an herbalist whose assortment of dried leaves, bark and roots could cure all ills. A perfumer with the marvelous fragrance of his essential oils and incense had his shop beside a jeweler displaying a cornucopia of precious gems. A whole street in one section was devoted only to storytellers. Above them all, on the upper floors, were the opium dens, infamous from Amsterdam to Bangkok.

Today, however, I was looking for the truck bazaar and the Rainbow Hotel. Instead of narrow streets lined with shops, in the truck bazaar the buildings formed a large courtyard about a city block square. Rising up out of the old motor oil and antifreeze in the center was the Rainbow Hotel. Five stories of whitewash reflected the afternoon sun, splashing the light like an ocean wave smashing upon a rock, sending sprays of reflected sun around the yard.

The whole enclosure was alive with activity. Different clans had staked out small areas to work and live in. To the left, young boys splashed and sprayed each other as they washed the family truck. To the right, a group of women knelt by small dung-fired stoves, cooking rice and dhal for the noon meal. Here trucks were repaired, painted and elaborately decorated. Trappings of silver and copper adorned the fenders and cabs, while murals told stories on the sides. The area's inhabitants defecated in the courtyard, for there were no official toilets. The challenge was to avoid all the puddles while weaving through the maze of trucks.

The Rainbow was arranged like a square doughnut with 50 or so rooms filling the outer edge, leaving the center an open mezzanine, from the lobby to the roof. I shared a third-floor, freshly whitewashed, 14-by-16-foot room with two Dutch men in their mid-20s and two other (currently sleeping) people occupying two of the six cots in the room. The Hollanders spoke a little English, so we engaged in conversation as travelers do when they find someone who speaks their language. I had been in that part of the world for nearly a year and rarely passed up a chance to speak English. I had lots of useful information for anyone heading east towards India, while they told me about the Netherlands and the latest news from Europe.

Several hours passed before the sleepers started to stir. First a girl, then a boy awoke and sat up as if they were surprised to hear voices in the room. The girl sleepily said her name was Anna in a thick German accent. He said nothing as he shuffled through a bag half under the bed.

"You guys want some morphine?" he said with the same thick German accent as Anna's.

"It's really good shit," chimed in Anna with the only spark of life I ever heard from her.

I said no thanks as a familiar pain stabbed at me. Growing up in the inner city, I was no stranger to these kinds of drugs. I had witnessed high school buddies turn purple and convulse because of heroin overdoses. I once found an old friend on a downtown street, shot, beaten and left for dead for ripping off the wrong person to get a fix. I saw young girls not much different than Anna become literal slaves because of heroin. The despair and degradation of hard drug usage I had already witnessed and wanted no part of. To my relief, the Dutch boys also turned down the offer.

The Germans did their needle ritual as junkies do and proceeded to vocally attack each other. Even in a foreign language, abuse is abuse. I quickly reached my tolerance of this scene and left to find a place to eat.

Several blocks away, I found a Punjabi restaurant that had a reasonably clean kitchen. There I feasted on samosas, sort of like crepes filled with mashed potatoes and green peas. After eating my fill, I took a walk around the city.

Exotic faces confronted me at every turn. There was the face of a holy man, calm and introspective. He lived on a desk-size space on the sidewalk. He cooked, slept and prayed on that same spot for years, never having to beg, for people always gave him what he needed. Then there were the dirty faces of beggar children pleading for a coin, and the stern, bearded face of a Mullah, absorbed in scripture one moment, then suddenly uttering a few words and chasing all the begging kids away. I saw eyes glistening behind the small crocheted eyeholes of the chitdoors that gave away no secrets of the tenants. I let all the faces, smells, sounds, animals, taxis, people, lights and beggars shower my senses until they became a high all their own.

I returned to my room feeling good with myself. Anna and her buddy were talking with another scruffy German junky friend. I could tell by his dead eyes and bare feet that he had stayed a little too long at the Rainbow. The three headed out for the "O" dens as I pulled a book from my pack and lay down on my cot. The Dutch travelers returned a little while later and soon went to sleep. I stayed up reading for a while; then I, too, fell asleep.

With a crash the door flew open and the light turned on. It was after midnight, and Anna and her buddy, back from the dens, were in the middle of a fight, as usual. I suddenly jumped up. Now I was yelling the loudest, telling them to "shut the f_ _k up," or I would personally deposit them and their belongings in the lobby without the benefit of the stairs.

To my surprise, it worked! Soon all was again quiet, leaving me to stare at the darkness, unable to go back to sleep. I was glad I was leaving in the morning and made a mental note never to stay at the Rainbow again.

At first light I awoke and began writing a letter. My attention was sidetracked by a faraway commotion that was growing louder as a crowd of people approached the corner of the building. It was then I heard another much more desperate sound: a guttural moan beyond screaming.

We all asked at once in several different languages, "What the hell is going on?"

I was first to the door and, quickly opening it, stepped into a crowd of onlookers. What I saw on that morning, halfway round the world, I will take to my grave. The scruffy junky that had been in my room the night before was being carried out of a nearby room, the flesh eaten off his feet.

He had stepped barefoot into something tasty on his way home from the opium den. As he slept the numb, opium sleep, rats had come and eaten their fill.

I left Peshawar later that morning, certain that running away from civilization might not be such a bad idea after all.

Can Can to Boulder

by Tom DuBois

MY FRIEND BOB AND I WERE OFF ON A ROAD TRIP from San Diego to Boulder to visit a college buddy at Colorado University and see the Rolling Stones. We headed through the Mojave Desert and on into Nevada in his Toyota Corolla. Driving overnight to avoid the blistering July heat in our non-air conditioned car made sense. I slept while Bob zipped past Las Vegas and entered southern Utah.

WHAM! I flew about a foot in the air.

"I think I just ran over a boulder or something," Bob told me. "It was right in the middle of the road. I couldn't avoid it." We continued, hoping the car was undamaged. Suddenly, the speedometer veered rapidly to the right, indicating the car was going over a hundred miles an hour. But we weren't. The car was actually slowing down. After coasting to a stop, I checked underneath the car and saw the rear axle had a large V in it where the car had struck the boulder at 80 mph. The V had pinched the axle and cut it in half.

Where were we? "Somewhere about 20 miles outside St. George, Utah," Bob said. Our map told us we were almost exactly half the way to Boulder and our watch told us it was 5:30 in the morning. Now what?

About 15 minutes later, a Utah state trooper pulled up. After insisting there were no boulders in the road for the last 10 miles (we know, we knocked it to the shoulder we wanted to say), he rudely asked Bob: "Well, would you have hit the boulder had it have been a human body?" The trooper called a tow truck to take our car to the town of Hurricane. (I wondered how a town in Utah could get that name!) The only garage that worked on "foreign cars" didn't open until nine, when the mechanic arrived to survey the damage and explain that the repair could easily be done in about a week, after the new axle arrived. The only solution was to walk out to Hurricane's main intersection with our thumbs up. The sun rose higher and our spirits sunk lower as car after car passed us. Bob turned to me and said, "I'm going to step in front of the next car that comes to this intersection and beg for a ride!"

Moments later an old pickup truck carrying a camper eased up to the intersection. Bob stepped out in front with his hands in a "halt" position. The surprised occupants of the truck, a couple in their 60s, came to a stop as Bob walked around to the driver's window and did, indeed, beg them for a ride up the interstate. After briefly listening to our woes, they offered to take us up the highway 150 miles. They had just returned from a trip to Zion National Park and told us all about it. Bob and I waved happily to them as they drove north and off, and we turned east to Colorado, via Interstate 70. The two of us had just set our bags down, anticipating a long stint of waiting, when another old pickup truck pulled over, kicking up gravel as it came to a dusty halt.

"Where ya headed?" asked a scruffy-looking guy about our age.

"Colorado," I said. Then came those words so sweet to the hitchhiking world.

"So am I!" he said, "Hop in, I'm on my way home to Boulder."

"God lives," thought Bob and I as we loaded our gear into the back of the truck and climbed into the cab. We were getting a 400-mile ride to our final destination. The guy offered us a beer from the beat-up cooler at our feet. After our ordeal in the desert sun, we eagerly accepted a cool one. Then he asked if we could open one for him. Bob handed him a can.

I hadn't even reached the halfway mark when he crushed his can, tossed it out the window and asked us to grab him another.

As our car sped through the red rocks of southern Utah, the driver went well over his legal limit. He wasn't swerving or weaving, just going way too fast, nearing 90 miles an hour. When Bob asked if he could help with the driving, he was brusquely rebuffed. I finally lost it when we barreled down a mountain pass at almost a hundred.

"Could you please slow down?" I nervously pleaded.

Finally, we stopped to refuel and calm our nerves. As our driver went into the gas station market, Bob and I considered the possibility that he'd tire out and one of us could take over before the highway patrol pulled him over or we crashed.

"Here, have one," our driver said while opening the first of two fresh six-packs and pulling out onto the highway. Bob and I came up with a new strategy. We drank as fast as possible to prevent him from binging on the remainder. It was a great strategy. He drove us safely and without incident all the way to Boulder, right up to the Sigma Nu fraternity house across the street from the University of Colorado.

I never got his name.

The Crossing

by Tom Turman

IT'S LATE ON THE LAST DAY OF A THREE-WEEK TRIP that Wal, his wife, Susan, and I are taking around West Africa. The three of us are returning to Ghana, where we live and teach at the University of Science and Technology. Our drive has taken us east from Ghana through Togo, Benin, Nigeria and up to Niger, across to Upper Volta and back down to Togo.

I jounce around the back seat of Wal's half-van/half-pickup VW as we rumble across the top of northern Togo toward the Ghanaian border crossing at Bawku. There is no town as Bawku, just a big gate or something. While it's getting late, we feel we can make it before sundown, the traditional time of border closure. Our party spent last night in a tin roofed schoolhouse trying to sleep through a rainstorm. The little room came alive with the tink-tank-banging of the big, African raindrops on the metal roof. It was like Chinese water torture all night, so we are not in great shape. All of us are tired of each other, hungry and eager to get home.

"I think we're there," Wal breaks into my thoughts. Everyone strains to see down the road. There is a six-foot-high grassy march on either side leading down to a crude, wooden pole let down across the road from a post on the right. Off to the left and up on a slight, sloped widening of the road is a thatch shack with no windows. This is the Togo side of the border crossing. There is no one in sight as we creep down the rutted, dirt road toward the flimsy wooden barrier.

"Lets just go around the gate and get over to the Ghanaian side," I say.

"No, we can't do that," Susan quickly says, peering up the hill at the shack on the hill. "We need the exit stamps, don't we?"

"I'm with Tom," Wal growls. "Let's just get out of here."

I can see smoke rising from the Ghanaian side of the border about a half a mile away. No one is at the Togo side.

Wal brings the VW to a stop a few feet from the wooden pole across the road and we get out. Wal and I are lifting the pole up when we hear the spring action of a rifle being loaded.

"STOP!" Two young soldiers are stumbling out of the shack, partially dressed and armed with an old M-1 rifle and a big Browning automatic. The one with the Browning can barely hold the big thing up. "You cannot go. Too late. Go back."

As one of the guards gets to us and lowers the pole, Wal says, "It isn't too late, the sun's not down yet."

"You give us a dash. Then go," one says in a drunken bravado.

"No. No money. This is an open border."

There is a pause as the skinny soldiers inch closer. The smell of booze is strong.

"GO BACK." They both emphasize this by pointing their weapons at us, then waving the barrels back up the

109

road. They are nervous and drunk, and the guns are shaking in their grip.

"It's two hours back to the last town. We can't go back." I am waving our passports at them.

"GO BACK!" they shout in unison.

Susan, tugging at our sleeves, says, "Let's just go back up the road and camp. We've got good food. We've even got some wine left. Come on, it's just one more day."

Even Wal and I realize we aren't getting anywhere with these two, so we back up 50 yards to the next widening and set up camp.

Later, after a bottle of wine and a good dinner, we are sitting around staring into the small fire. It is about time for sleep.

Suddenly, the two border guards lurch around the rear end of the VW shouting, "WE SEARCH. WE SEARCH. UP. UP," and they jerk their rifle barrels up in the air, then back down at us.

The soldier with the M-1 lifts the corner of the tarp covering our stuff in the back of the VW and peers in. "WE SEARCH. OPEN UP," he shouts again.

Wal and I look at each other just long enough to agree on a silent plan. Each of us grabs a corner of the tarp and pulls the cover back toward the cab. When the two soldiers lean in and start to grab things, Wal and I swoop the canvas up and back over them. The weight of the wet canvas cover knocks them down near the fire.

Angry and frustrated, we jump on the shrieking, flailing canvas bundle and hit everything that moves with whatever we have grabbed. The struggling finally stops. Wal and I are lying winded on the inert, canvas-covered lump. Wal menacingly clutches a two-foot wheel of cheese while

I have been hitting them with a long, hard salami. Susan's face cannot be described.

As we whip the tarp off, the fire flares, lighting up the two dazed soldiers. While Wal bends over close to their faces, yelling in their ears, I gather up the guns and break them down, putting all the parts together in a sack. I throw the sack at the nearest one knocking him into the other one.

"Get out and don't come back," we yell together.

The two scared soldiers stagger out of the firelight, dragging their sack of weapons.

Wal grabs the last bottle of wine and takes a long pull. Then he sits down next to Susan, who pronounces, "Way to go, tough guys. Who the hell do you think we're going to face tomorrow morning?"

"Oh, c'mon, they were robbing us. I'm not taking it any more," is all Wal can say.

"Maybe we should make a run for it now. Just go through and take our chances on the Ghana side," I suggest.

We repack the VW and stand around the fire discussing our options. It is then that we all notice the three sets of headlights weaving and bouncing toward us from the Ghanaian direction. Our options have just disappeared.

Two jeeps and an old black Mercedes fill the road next to our campsite. Several Ghanaian soldiers surround us while one dramatically opens the rear door of the Mercedes. An officer with a shaved head steps out and grunts something in his language. Two soldiers push us up to the bald man. He is a colonel.

"You have shown no respect for authority," and he points to the two drunk Togo soldiers he has brought with him. "You must be smugglers bringing contraband into my country. You are under arrest." He folds himself back into the black car, grunting just before the door closed, "Bring them."

Wal is to drive our car between the jeeps. The lead jeep takes Susan and me across to the Ghanaian military compound. It is 2 a.m. when we arrive, too late for any interrogation. Each of us is put in separate cells to worry and wait alone. There is only the clinking of the keys for a few moments as the guard leaves the crude cellblock.

"Thanks for the nice trip and good night, boys," Susan sings sarcastically from her cell. Neither of us answers.

The next morning breakfast is served, tea and a spicy mush with bread. Then each of us is brought separately to the bald colonel's office for interrogation. This goes on all morning. Glancing through the windows I notice that soldiers are methodically taking apart our VW in their search for contraband.

Finally all three of us are brought before the officer. "This is our sovereign border, and we are here to protect it. You come to our countries and think you can do anything you want. When soldiers give you orders you must obey."

"We're just going back home. Those guys over there were drunk. They were robbing us. Doesn't that count for anything?"

The colonel ignores this. "If I find any contraband in your vehicle you will go to prison. Do you understand?"

"What do you mean by contraband?" I ask.

"Military equipment or weapons. Explosives. Written material calling for the fall of the government. I shall be the judge. I have been trained in America and I have trained my men well. They will find any illegal material you have hidden."

There is a noisy commotion in the yard outside the window. A soldier holding a box up high over his head breaks from the group dismantling our car and we all watch him scurry toward us. Soon, there is a rap at the door.

"Come."

The soldier triumphantly bursts into the room with a handful of Susan's Tampons clutched in his hand. The strings of the white, cotton cylinders drape over his black hand like the wicks of dynamite sticks. "Bomb, sir," he announces proudly. "We have found bombs." With a flourish he spreads the Tampons on the astounded colonel's desk. The frowning officer, visibly shocked, jerks away from the pile of menstrual devices and with an angry grunt orders the soldier out.

"Is that about it, colonel, or would you like to light one of these and see what happens," Susan says, covering for the two of us laughing behind her.

"GET OUT AND DON'T COME THROUGH HERE AGAIN."

Uh-Oh, Silver

by Nola M. Dunbar

OUTDOOR WEDDINGS CAN BE HARD WORK. Particularly when you're trying to get organized in a thunderstorm. Often, there is no time to grab an umbrella as the dark clouds thicken and bad luck pours down. We believe everything is under control only to discover everything is controlling us.

This is particularly true when the groom happens to be our son, Chad. When he finished high school, the lights went out during the graduation ceremony. Battling my way to the exit, a tornado passed near the school and then bisected our farm like a John Deere bulldozer. When Chad headed to the beach for a graduation celebration, our region was shaken by a mild earthquake. This was strange because North Carolina doesn't have earthquakes. During his outdoor graduation from college in May, 1997, a cold rain added a chilling note to the festivities. Once when helping his uncle in the tobacco fields, he stepped on a six-foot rattlesnake. I hoped that as the wedding day drew near, his luck would improve. I should have known better.

Alston, my husband of 32 years, was home cooking the rehearsal dinner feast while I ferried food and completed the setup and cleanup work. Since the honeymoon would take place in the fall, Chad and his bride, Samantha, decided that the family could accompany them on a week-long postnuptial celebration in Cherokee, North Carolina. A family vacation in a rented cabin would be perfect.

But first we had to get through the wedding. Working hard on a sweltering May day, my sister-in-law finished the yard wedding decorations with bows, netting, flowers and table arrangements. Even the tent and tables for the post-wedding pig picking looked elegant.

When she arrived for the wedding rehearsal dinner, Samantha gave us a great smile. A day earlier her orthodontist had removed her braces and affixed temporary front teeth implants. Her big grin was aimed at Chad. Unfortunately the temporary tooth had fallen out. All was well again after an emergency trip to her orthodontist.

The wedding day was perfect. No hail, no earthquakes, no haze and the temperature an ideal 70 degrees. As Chad, his brother, Trey, Alston and the preacher waited for the wedding party, someone shouted: "No one can get lost in Beaufort County." After a few calls, wrong turns and a flat tire, the flower girl and her party showed up an hour late.

Despite the delay the wedding was a delight. Fortunately the thunderstorms didn't hit until after we began dismantling the decorations. Despite all the midnight twists and turns up and down the narrow roads, our family trip to the rented cabin was effortless. Sunrise brought a breathtaking view as the hazy fog topped the valley.

Alston talked Chad and Samantha into a whitewater rafting trip. A poor swimmer, I gave my regrets, "You're not getting me in any raft after last night's storm. I'll tour the Indian museum instead."

Hours later, they returned with a hair-raising tale of Chad being thrown from the raft into the roiling river. Now it was time for a peaceful horseback ride down the side of the mountain. Chad booked the first trip of the day.

"We know nothing about horses; is this safe?" I asked our instructor. I learned that the horses were gentle enough for a child. After a one-minute introductory lesson we saddled up and rode into the woods.

Our guide led the way. Camera dangling from his neck, Chad followed astride Silver, his graceful appaloosa. I followed on my mount, sure-footed Chief. Samantha trailed behind me. Bringing up the rear was Old Buck who had begun biting his rider, Alston.

We halted in a small clearing as our guide prepared for a steep descent down the narrow, winding mountain trail. Samantha's horse nudged and pushed Chief's rear end. Chief started pressing forward to beat Chad and Silver down the trail. Old Buck pushed forward while continuing to sink his teeth into Alston, an old jet jock who loves spitting in the face of danger and can't see this horse getting the better of him.

Then Old Buck started bucking, which led Samantha's horse to flip her off the saddle. After Samantha hit the side of a tree, my horse tried to stomp Samantha's head into the ground. Whimpering and crying, Samantha curled around the tree for protection.

Now Silver was trying to break loose and fly down the mountainside. "Jump off," the guide yelled to Chad, who leapt as his foot caught in the stirrup. After his head and camera hit the ground, he finally managed to free his foot. Our guide jumped from his horse and tried to gain control.

"Calm down, Chief. It's all right. Calm down, boy." Then turning to me he yelled, "Jump off."

"I can't, I need help," I replied. I finally managed to get down safely to the ground.

Suddenly Old Buck, eager to join the fun, reared up and bolted through the forest.

"Help me!" Samantha moaned, as Chad and I helped her up and back toward the corral.

"You can have all your money back," yelled the guide.

Suddenly Buck came galloping out of the woods with Alston still hanging on.

"He backed me down the edge of the mountain and tried to knock me off," shouted Alston. "I've been afraid two times in my life, and this was one of 'em. I like having control of things and that horse took it away."

"Those horses been penned up almost two weeks without a walkin' cause of the rains," the ticket man said while handing us our refund.

We rode home on a train without incident. Samantha broke into a smile that looked great, even though her front tooth was missing again.

Playing My Last Card

by Elizabeth Mullet

CREDIT CARD COMPANIES HATE ME. I only carry one card and pay my bill on time. I never rack up any interest. How un-American is that? Leaving home on a four-week trip to South America, I signed a check and asked my parents to pay the bill as soon as it arrived. I was en route to Paraguay to help a friend serving as a volunteer nurse at a primitive clinic.

Eager to see friends along the way, I made the 15-hour trip from North Carolina to Miami by car. I had arranged to park at a friend's house in Homestead, a short distance from the Miami airport. He offered to drive me to the airport. When I arrived at his house, already behind schedule because of wrong directions, my friend was missing. I was greeted by a woman who said, "He asked me to tell you that he had to go somewhere and won't be back in time to take you to the airport. But you are welcome to leave your car."

A taxi to the airport would cost $50. The parking garage at the airport probably wouldn't charge much more than $100, I reasoned.

I drove.

The daily parking fee at the airport was $10. Surprisingly there were no posted monthly rates. But I knew that longer-term rental would be discounted. Besides I was already late for my flight. Without double-checking the price, I parked and rushed to my plane.

The trip was great. As a nurse I was delighted to use my experience to help make a difference in Paraguay. And I remembered to call home to remind my parents to pay my credit card bill. The month went by quickly, but the trip home was slowed by a 12-hour delay due to mechanical problems.

During a layover in Bolivia, I noticed that my right eye was very itchy. By 7 a.m., it was swollen almost completely shut.

After sitting up for 27 hours, I finally arrived in Miami. When I handed in my parking slip, a big $300 appeared on the screen. My good eye blinked. There was no discount for longer-term parking. I handed over my only card.

The attendant swiped it and studied the screen. "Denied," he announced flatly.

"What does that mean?"

"It's denied! You don't have enough money in there!" he snarled.

"That can't be!" I sputtered. "I have a $2,000 limit and I hardly put a thing on there."

"I don't care, it's denied. You'll have to find some other way to pay."

I had been planning to pay for my trip home with that credit card. I only had a little cash, plus a few traveler's checks and two personal checks with me. "Can I pay you with a personal check?" I asked desperately.

He nodded.

I filled out the check and handed it over. He looked at it a little, fiddled around and then said, "I can't take a check for the whole amount. Give me a check for $150 and the rest in cash."

"I don't *have* $150 in cash. Can I give you traveler's checks?"

He agreed. I handed over my traveler's checks and my last personal check. Then I called my credit card company and learned that even if I immediately transferred money to my card it would remain invalid another 24 hours.

I needed to get to my doctor, 15 hours away by car. Although I was exhausted there was no way I could stop to rest.

"Lord," I cried, "I can't do it. Please help me." The toll-gate bar lifted and I drove out into the Miami sunshine.

Although I usually drink Mountain Dew to stay awake, I was afraid to spend money for anything besides gas. I had plenty of water and thought, "If Jesus can turn water into wine, He can make water work like Mountain Dew."

Just as Moses parted the Red Sea, the Lord decided to clear the interstate for my long journey. Miraculously, there was no congestion except for a tiny hitch near Ft. Lauderdale. When I arrived home I had been awake for more than 44 hours. The flora and fauna were simply amazing. At one point I saw a shadow buffalo jumping across the road and started to brake until I reminded myself that there were no buffalo in North Carolina. And as I turned the last sharp curve, en route to my home, there was a nice tall coconut palm tree growing by the road. Funny, it hadn't been there when I left a month earlier.

As I pulled into my driveway that night I realized the Lord truly was my shepherd. Going through my mail the next day I discovered two credit card bills my parents failed to recognize by the return address. I have since signed up for several more. And today, whenever I head for the road, I always make sure that I'm well stocked with Mountain Dew.

The Non-Stop Mini

by Ethel F. Mussen

"Tua matricula! Matricula!" demanded the man in uniform. I could not tell whether it was a policeman or soldier who had stepped out of the woods to confront me.

Assuming he wanted to know if the car was stolen, I reached for the rental papers in the glove compartment. He shook his head. "No, no. *La matricula!*" he repeated.

I guessed then that he wanted my driver's license, but it was in my purse. He gestured, miming the turn of the ignition key.

I protested, "No, no. *No puedo!* I can't stop!" At last I found the license. The officer looked it over and then waved me on, shaking his head in amusement at the woman who wouldn't turn off her car.

The truth was that I couldn't stop unless someone was around to give me a push and get me going again.

After a four-day workshop in Lisbon, I had set out to tour Portugal on my own. At the hotel I arranged for an economy vehicle just big enough for my suitcase and me. The two-door red Mini Morris Minor caught my fancy and off I went to Obidos, the queen's private village.

By dusk I chugged up the one-way street that ascended the hill and passed under an arch lined with the Portuguese blue tiles I had come to see. In the village center, just beyond the arch, I parked before a scarlet bougainvillea vine that draped the entrance to a small hotel restaurant. The friendly mustachioed bar man informed me regretfully that they were full, but he'd call someone just below the village to see about a room.

I was in luck; they'd house me. My Mini coughed a little, then the engine turned over and I glided down to a rustic B&B just past the bottom of the hill.

The next morning, I started up to the village to see who answered the call of the Sunday morning church bells. Unfortunately the car was less eager than I to go back up the hill. It snorted, whined and died. My B&B host and his stout, laughing wife panted and pushed from behind and rolled me along the driveway to the road. At last the engine caught and after a brief run to test it, I wound around and back up to the bougainvillea.

The vested bar man and two customers in full suits stood at the door watching the Sunday morning parade into church. One shop was open and I found exactly the sort of ceramic bowl I'd been seeking. I bought a crocheted shawl to pad it and a long, linen tablecloth to set it on. Elated with my discovery, I stashed my purchase beside my suitcase and turned the key to start up.

The engine wheezed, sighed and died. Had I flooded it? I waited, then tried again with no luck. Inside the hotel, I appealed for help. The customers and bartender carefully removed their jackets and decided that if I coasted downhill the engine would pick up again. A big push helped the Mini glide over the crest. Suddenly, a donkey cart emerged from a house below and clopped slowly into the middle of the road. I clutched the wheel as the car gathered speed, zoomed around the cart at the bottom without hitting a house and swerved into the rutted road, just as the engine sputtered and caught. I sped on to Nazare and the colorful fishing boats without further incident.

Mini coughed but started the next morning and I headed inland, passing village fountains where gossiping women were filling pitchers and ollas. I dared not stop for pictures. Traffic was moderate; the Mini hummed along. I decided it was the victim of dirty gasoline clogging the carburetor or maybe a flywheel problem that I would report when I turned it in. I made it to Figueira da Foz by late afternoon. The palatial hotel was empty except for one other couple.

The next morning, after a leisurely walk across the broad beach to the sea, it was time to head back to Lisbon to avoid rush-hour traffic on the major highway into the city.

Mini Morris did not choose to leave. Fortunately a garage was only a block away, but the owner had gone home for lunch and was in no hurry to return since the town was hardly teeming with customers.

At 2:30 p.m. he appeared, but finding the problem and repairing it would require an overnight stay. When I declined this solution, he offered to push me along the wide road to get the car started and then recommended that I scurry back to Lisbon. We made two passes along that thoroughfare, once north, once south, to make sure that the engine would continue running after it started and I was on my way.

After the chance encounter with the uniform who demanded to see my license, I barreled along the highway without pausing, bypassing the towns with their Roman ruins and tombs of kings, until I neared Lisbon. From the vineyards, trucks loaded with the grape harvest joined the increasing traffic, and the two lanes south toward the city filled with stop-and-go drivers. The road stretched steadily downhill, which favored my little beast, but there was never enough space between cars to let it pick up speed if it died again. Mini and I sweated out the pause-and-roll regime.

My arms and legs grew stiff as we inched forward into Lisbon. Through signals and roundabouts we kept rolling. I recalled thankfully that the car return was just off the highway. I pulled into the garage, staggered to the desk, reported that the car had difficulty starting and paid my bill. A cab took me to my hotel and the next day I left. The airplane flew smoothly without coughing, sputtering or stalling all the way to London.

Look Both Ways on Small Islands

by Linda Ballou

A SOLID RAP ON THE DOOR OF THE COTTAGE I shared with three other Club Med guests on the island of Moorea in Tahiti startled me. I peeked through the cracks in the thatched door to see two official-looking men in khaki shorts and green shirts, holsters strapped on their hips. The tallest gendarme's gun was barely visible beneath a belly pushing hard on the buttons of his sweat-stained shirt. His partner fondled the handle of his weapon as they stood in the tropical sun waiting for my response. I recognized a third, sun-burnished man in shorts, a T-shirt and sandals to be an employee of the club.

"What is it?" I asked from behind the door.

"They want to look in your luggage," said the employee, who was apparently there to interpret for the French-speaking officers.

"What are they looking for?"

"Cannabis," he said

My heart fibrillated. "Cannabis . . .. I don't have any cannabis," I stammered.

I may have eaten the stuff in a brownie, used it instead of oregano in spaghetti sauce, but I would never be foolish enough to carry it in my luggage across international borders. I swung the door wide and invited the men in to proclaim my innocence.

The corpulent officer, beads of sweat on his upper lip, pawed through my luggage. His friend, with the darting eyes of a rat, scanned my belongings. They were not even the tiniest bit interested in my roommate's luggage. They only searched mine.

The overstuffed version of the law lifted my bra high in the air to examine it carefully. He actually sniffed it and smiled in my direction. His compatriot giggled.

"See, no cannabis," I said.

There was an exchange between the G.O. and the gendarmes in French. (I never knew for sure what G.O. stands for in Club Med language, but I think it means "gorgeous only" need apply.)

"They want you to come with them," the G.O. said.

"What for? They can see I don't have anything."

"They want to ask you some questions."

They were rounding up the usual suspects. "Okay," I said, knowing I had nothing hidden in my bikini.

They took me to a cramped cubicle on the club grounds cooled by an overhead fan. The heavy-set officer lit up a cigarette and blew the smoke between the large spaces between his front teeth into my face. I felt I'd been shanghaied into a scene from Casablanca.

"What do you do?" the bra sniffer asked me through the interpreter.

"I sell real estate in Los Angeles," I said feeling very much like a "Lost Angel" that day. "Why?"

"Just answer their questions," the G.O. warned me. "These guys can put you in a French jail and throw away the key."

"Who were you talking to on the island yesterday?"

Yesterday. I tried to remember that far back. The first

leg of the two-week trip was spent on the remote island of Bora Bora. I shared the tranquility there with a dozen guests and a handful of Club Med crew. My thatched hut set on poles in the water overlooked the clear water of a placid lagoon. All guests were herded onto a sailboat and taken to a sandy spit in the sun where we spent the afternoon. After lunch we were given free rein to explore the tiny, palm-studded paradise. I moseyed away from the rest of the guests getting juiced on what the G.O.' s affectionately refer to as "gasoline." I recalled stumbling across three semi-naked, casual types, lying on the sand. They had arrived in a zodiac, off of a yacht, anchored about a half-mile out in the bay. They could speak English and were smoking the devil weed, cannabis. They offered me a puff. I declined and continued on to the tip of a sand spit to contemplate the powdery white earth, tickling breeze and dozen shades of blue stacked to the horizon.

That evening, while drying my hair in the soft light of the golden hour, I heard a hissing sound from the shrubbery. It was the local boy in day-glow sneakers I had danced with the night before in the outdoor pavilion.

"Will you trade me beads for money?" he whispered. The club had its own currency of plastic pop beads that guests wore around their neck allowing them to be free from all material cares, like purses and wallets. The local boy wanted to go dancing that night and to be able to buy his fair share of gasoline. I saw no harm in trading him $10 worth of beads. I handed a bag full of the baubles over the porch rail and he gave me a 10-spot in exchange. This incident flashed through my mind just as the G.O. asked me, "What did you give the boy last night?"

The two French officers never took their eyes away,

calculating my every move as they awaited my answers. Doughboy had a profoundly hooked nose, bulbous wet lips and a black bar across the top of his face for eyebrows. His gaze never went higher than my cleavage. The rat-faced officer was a slat-ribbed bandy rooster with spindly legs that he kept crossed. He bobbed one booted foot incessantly. Saliva sprayed as he spoke in excited French to his porky counterpart.

"I traded some beads for money." I said looking down, afraid that they did not believe a word I was saying.

They kept asking me the same questions over and over, trying to trip me up in a lie. The gendarmes grilled me for over an hour.

"What is it they think I've done?" I finally asked the G.O. through welling tears of exasperation.

"They think you are a marijuana mule on your way back to California. They busted a yacht in the harbor last night and seized bales of the stuff. They saw you talking to the people who were on that boat."

"Good grief! What are they going to do with me?" I asked, really scared now.

"They could deport you," he said.

"I don't know anything about any cannabis," I blubbered. "I'm innocent. I'm just a silly tourist who maxed out her credit card for a couple of weeks in paradise." My lips quivered as I pleaded. "Please don't deport me. I'll never get my money back, and I'll never get to be here again."

"Did you kiss him?" rodent face asked me in English.

"Kiss who?" I demanded, angry that they had concealed they could speak English just to terrify me.

"The boy last night," he sniggered.

"No!" I said. "And so what if I did?" When they both

broke into broad smiles, I knew the interrogation was over.

"You can go," the rooster crowed. The men doubled over, convulsed with laughter as I ran out of their lair and headed straight for the bar where I planned to guzzle a few gallons of gasoline. A case of the shakes in the morning would be a small price to pay to obliterate this session from my mind.

Mexican Madness

by Marilou Brewer

It isn't that far. I mean, come on, Mom, I live in Southern California and we are only going to Mexico. It's practically next door and four of us are going in two cars. Ray, Stephanie, Don and me. Ray just inherited a fortune and he wants to take us all. I know it's my first trip, but I'm old enough and I promise I'll be careful. Honest I will.

So off the four of us went. Two guys. Two gals. This was my very first trip out of the country. Heading south to Mexico's beautiful beaches felt great. What could be better? Mazatlan, San Blas, Puerto Vallarta. Wonderful names. Dream stuff for a child of the late '60s.

We were on the road and traveling well. Cabin tent. Oriental rugs. Trunks full of colorful clothes. Heaven on a shoestring. Driving, driving, driving in shifts all the way down to Mazatlan. Parked at last and right on the beach. Paradise.

Our first stop was the tourist office where we could get safe water. Much to our surprise, the tourist agents told us that the water coming from the spigot on the front of the building was perfectly safe. Naturally, we filled our five-gallon jugs.

Four days later, the first fellow fell. Amoebic dysentery. The next day, the second one surrendered and was soon hospitalized. We gals became instant nurses right down to the IVs. Two weeks, countless hospital bills and two extended hotel stays later, our group traveled on to San Blas.

En route, I came down with typhoid fever at 3 a.m. By 9, we were lying on the beach. I had a fever of 105.5, was delirious, shaking and sweating. Time for my hospitalization. It would have been a lot easier if I spoke Spanish.

A couple of weeks later, our group was in Puerto Vallarta camping on Mismaloya Beach right next to the recently abandoned movie set for *Night of the Iguana.* Every time I ate, I got sick all over again. It was time to find an American doctor.

On arrival in Guadalajara. Stephanie and Ray, who were paying for this fiasco, flew off to Los Angeles and left Don and I camped in a trailer park in Guadalajara with $50. They were going to be back in a couple of days. They just went home to pick up more cash.

Two weeks later, we realized they weren't coming back. Our American doctor suggested I call home. Typhoid fever was more serious than I realized. Mom said she would get on the horn and find Ray and Stephanie. They were in their new Hollywood apartment, buying furniture and making a home for their new Great Dane puppy.

Fifty dollars doesn't go very far, even in Mexico in the '60s.

Best way to both cope and get well? Sleep. And I did . . . ad nauseum. I woke up while Don was off taking out the trash and stumble-bumbled into the clean white tile bathroom a couple of doors away. Next thing I knew he was sitting next to me saying, "Oh, no, Lou. Oh, no." I was lying on my face in my white dress on the white tile floor in a pool of bright red blood. I lifted my head and started spitting out pieces of my lovely, well-cared-for teeth. I had passed out getting up from the john and just went straight over face first. Seven stitches to the chin, four to the eyebrow, 12 shattered teeth. We called Ray and Stephanie at 8 o'clock that night to tell them.

At 8 the next morning they walked into our tent. I was going to fly home immediately. Wrong. Due to a paperwork mix up, the American Embassy had failed to approve our new visa applications, and we couldn't leave on a commercial flight. Stephanie and I decided to charter a private plane to Tijuana and walk across the border. It would only cost us $500 for the seven-hour trip.

Nine-and-a-half hours later our makeshift air ambulance crash-landed out of gas on somebody's rancho 20 miles southeast of Mexicali. We hitched a ride in a Chevy with fuzzy dice and dingle balls in the windows all the way to the border. Mexico lets us out. U.S. Customs says, "Do you have anything to declare?

"Yes, I have a gun," says Stephanie.

"Where?" says the officer.

"It's dismantled on the top of my suitcase and the shells are on the bottom under the clothes."

We were immediately arrested for "transporting a concealed weapon across an international border." In the station they began to grill us. Everything came out of our suitcases. Even the linings. I was denied permission to go to the bathroom, until finally, the officers relented. As I sauntered back into the office, I saw Stephanie standing on her chair crying and yelling, "You leave her alone! She has typhoid fever!"

The customs teams dropped the suitcases and the charges and rushed us in a screaming ambulance out to El Centro County Hospital, where we spent the night in the all-cement psycho ward. Moaning came from the cell on my left. A weird small courtroom was on my right. What is *that* for? The next morning they moved us first thing into a ward across from the premature babies. Stephanie passed the typhoid test. I flunked.

When the hospital staff refused to let us phone home we staged a protest. "WE WANT A PHONE CALL! WE WANT A PHONE CALL," we screamed in the middle of the hall.

We flew back that night. I embarked on two dental surgeries to remove 12 shattered teeth. The typhoid treatments took months.

Our Honeymoon Was a Wreck

by Candace Hisert

HONEYMOONS ARE GREATLY OVERRATED. That's what my mother told me a week before my wedding. She also told me to let my husband handle all money matters and make all of the major decisions.

Of course that was in 1968. Times have changed, haven't they?

George and I were married in Chicago in December. The temperature was below zero. I dreamed of sunshine and palm trees, but when we arrived in the Azores it was raining. We had, it seems, flown in six months ahead of the sun.

At the grand hotel in Ponta Delgada, things began to improve. Our room had a canopy bed and marble floors. It was a mite chilly, but the gracious manager not only sent up a space heater, he also invited us to be his guests at the hotel's New Year's Eve party. He also suggested we take a drive to the other end of the island and see the big casino.

We had no money to gamble, but we thought we might splurge on a rental car and see the sights. At the only agency in town we picked the one car we could afford: a VW Beetle. George was not thrilled that the car lacked both pep and seatbelts, but at least it had stopped raining. We wanted an adventure. We drove out of town and up into the hills.

I remember hitting the pineapple truck. George remembers nothing. We were on a narrow stretch of mountain road, came around a corner and came upon the truck dead ahead. George hit the brakes. No brakes. There was no place to go except into the truck or over a cliff. Somehow, George managed to spin the wheel so that our car collided with the truck's tire.

We spent the rest of the honeymoon in the hospital. At least we got the same room. I had a broken wrist, cuts around the eye, an almost-severed ear, a bad knee and huge bruises. George had broken almost everything and had gone through the windshield and back again.

Amazingly, almost everyone who could speak English on the island came to our hospital room with presents. We had a steady stream of visitors including the American consul and an Irish nun, who brought us prayers and a pineapple. On New Year's Eve the chief doctor at the hospital stopped in on his way to the hotel's party. Elegantly dressed in evening clothes, the doctor brought a bottle of champagne and three glasses and insisted we drink a toast. I drank to our future. The present was too painful.

We still take a romantic vacation once a year. We rent mid-sized cars that come with everything. We try to avoid rainy seasons. And we always tell people we're on our honeymoon.

The Omen

by Carla Perry

A SUMMER STORM BLEW ACROSS THE FLATLANDS OF IOWA and toppled the Dutch elm in my neighbor's yard the morning of our departure for a trip to San Francisco. From the window, we could see our 1969 Jeepster Commando trapped under the branches. But we were determined to take this road trip, a two-week camping vacation, to rescue our marriage, to take the pressure off.

Two days before, on the way to get an extra gas tank welded to the Jeep, my husband drove into a pothole. The jolt caused a tire to blow. His bicycle, which he planned to use to get to work and had placed in the back, bounced and knocked out the Jeep's rear window. If it had not been my car and my husband, I would have laughed.

No one in town carried a replacement for the blown tire, which meant buying four new ones. On his way back from replacing the back window, my husband rented a chainsaw to remove the Jeep from the tree limbs. He called out to me: "The signs sure say, 'Don't Go. Don't Do It.'"

A friend who had borrowed our sleeping bags and was supposed to be back a week earlier still hadn't returned by morning. Nevertheless, this was our departure day. This was our vacation. This was our marriage.

As the sun set the first day out, cars blinked us down even though our lights were on low beam. We pulled off the highway and drove to a repair shop, to have the left front headlight adjusted. After merging back onto Interstate 80 our car was passed by a Cadillac that kicked up gravel and broke the same headlight.

We stopped for the night in the Cuba, New Mexico, outback and woke to frozen drinking water. Cold is a drag, especially without sleeping bags. It was time to head into town to buy long johns. The outfits came in handy during our two nights in Kingman, Arizona, waiting for a new alternator and regulator that had expired in the desert.

Old Iowa friends were waiting for us in San Francisco. Or so we thought. They had recently separated. "Don't go, please stay," the husband asked us over dinner in Chinatown. "Let's go home," I said, "back to Iowa. This is no fun."

On the way back, somewhere between Laramie and Cheyenne, Wyoming, we woke to my birthday, the fall equinox and a blizzard. Cresting a hill coated with ice, my husband swerved to avoid a Volkswagen Bug straddling both lanes. The Jeep's left front tire caught on snow piled on the side of the road, spun, flipped, slid, then rolled down an embankment. Our wood-splitting hatchet fell blade-first into the console between us. Then the Jeep rolled again.

By now the U-Haul car-top carrier was flattened, the windshield shattered, and the chassis magnificently askew. Since we had no car insurance, there was no need to call the police or file an accident report. Two young men stopped to help us gather our possessions, which had been flung from the spinning vehicle. I was still wearing sandals.

I found the car keys. In the snow.

My husband switched the Jeep into four-wheel drive.

And the ignition started!

After backing out of the ditch and onto the interstate, my spouse drove 900 miles home to Iowa, nonstop, afraid to shut off the car in case it would never start again.

The Dutch elm was still straddling the front yard and the driveway when we pulled up to the house. The telephone was ringing as we stumbled. It was my sister, placing her one call from a Missouri jail. She needed me to come down and bail her out. She was in St. Louis for the weekend and had been charged with a felony. There had been a police sting at a friend's radio station. Could I drive down and bring her home? I told her we had other plans.

Hipstress in Manhattan

by Laura Deutsch

FORTUNATELY, I WAS WEARING BLACK when I arrived at the hip Hudson Hotel in Manhattan. They let me check in even though I was over 35 and didn't sport the de rigeur butter-soft black leather jacket.

No awning, no name, no number. This place was so exclusive I didn't even know I'd arrived. A horizontal slash of chartreuse glass on a limestone facade and chic guests waiting on the sidewalk for cabs were the only clues. Threaded among them, handsome 20-something bellmen whispered into walkie-talkie wristwatches, cocking their heads to pick up responses.

A spot for "anyone and everyone who embraces style as a way of life," said owner Ian Schrager. In a move to keep the hotel "democratic," he'd set aside a few rooms at just $95 a night.

In my never-ending search for the perfect combination of hip and straight, I'd reserved one of these rooms. The Mark, my usual retreat when I flew in from California, was feeling too formal with its polished white marble lobby. What's more, the Mark's prices made $95 a night seem like a tip. At the hip Hudson, *Sex and the City* meets *Men in Black*. Beautiful people posed in the dimly lit lobby, as if waiting for a casting call. Stiff-suited businessmen, on hand for meetings, shifted awkwardly from one wing tip to the other.

The charming young bellman who showed me to my room was an actor when not handling luggage. Most of the staff were in the arts, he said, hired without hotel experience, so as not to be jaded.

My pleasure faded when I entered the room—so small the dark board and batten walls closed in on me as I sidled around the bed, banging my shin. Like Gulliver at the Hotel Lilliput, when I sat on the bed (no room for a chair), I could practically open the bedroom window with my left hand while turning on the bathroom shower with my right.

I closed my eyes to reconnect with the hip parts of myself.

Opening my eyes, I admired the minimalist style. A smooth white cotton duvet cover, no bedspread. Just like my bed at home, assuming these were 380-count Italian sheets. But my room at home has an Oriental carpet on its hardwood floor, an antique Japanese tansu, a monotype by a rising young artist and antique woodblock prints. The perfect combination of hip and straight.

The artfulness of the hotel room impressed me—a sheer white curtain on the wall between bed and bath, exotic hardwood floors and cool, industrial packaging for shampoo and body lotion. But another part of me whispered, "There are no drawers or shelves."

I wondered where to put the suitcase I'd have to live out of for a week.

"Is there a luggage rack?" I asked the bellman.

"What's a luggage rack?" he asked.

The rack, once found, could barely be wedged into the room. Squeezing it into a tiny, doorless closet niche, I showed the bellman how to set it up, which left no space to hang clothes.

Fun in my mini-room never stopped. When a burly engineer came to repair the hand-painted bedside lamp, he had to lie on the bed, his face in my pillows, to reach the plug.

I checked out some of the larger rooms, thinking I might upgrade, even at Republican prices. Some had closets and shelves, as well as small, tight, white leather settees. All rooms, no matter what size, had the same hard edge, no cush.

At 8 the next morning, I came down to the lobby in an elevator pounding out music I wasn't hip enough to recognize. A mix of heavy metal and punk, with a generous dollop of nerve-racking.

"Isn't this fabulous?" a bellman gushed. "We have music in the elevators now!"

The broad-shouldered German frau who rode down with me gripped a tweed lapel, tensing her jaw.

"How did you end up here?" I asked this 50ish woman who couldn't pretend she was searching for her perfect blend of hip and straight.

"A shtupit travel agent!" she barked. "He knows notink."

I stepped out into the lobby where rock music pulsed 24/7.

Sometimes you just have to throw in the hotel towel. I'll take my cutting edge slightly dulled, I decided. The Upper West Side is hip enough for me. And I'm flexible enough to slide between the covers at a nice Upper East Side boutique hotel, if required.

The next morning, I asked one of the bellmen to whisper into his watch and hail me a cab. The doorman at the Mark on 77th and Madison, in his black, caped greatcoat, opened my taxi door, then took my bags from the trunk. As I approached the front desk, I admired the shiny white marble.

The polite European desk clerk gave me my usual room. I crossed the plush carpet, past the king-size bed and sat on the cushy down couch. The right combination of hip and straight gets straighter with each passing year. And when I find the right balance, I intend to enjoy it from the comfort of an overstuffed sofa.

Young and Naïve in Morocco

by Rachel Seed

TAKEN WITH POETIC VISIONS of lazing around exotic cafés and being waited on hand and foot while drinking tea and scribbling letters under a canopy of brilliantly blue sky, my friend Sean and I set out for Morocco.

We set sail on a two-hour ferry ride from Algeciras, Spain, to Tangier. On arrival the two of us were surrounded by tour guides offering to show us the hidden joys of Tangier. "Where is it you want to go?" a man named Mohammed asked. "Shopping? To the hotel?" He found us decent lodging and then led us on to one of the best views in the city—the terrace of an open-air McDonald's.

Next he persuaded us to shop with merchants that were obviously close friends. "This is student price, student price," he assured Sean and me as we bought rugs for $50 apiece.

As dusk approached, Mohammed led the way to a dingy, tiled café where we lounged with his drug-dealing friend puffing on hash cigarettes and sipping sugary mint tea. The friend leered at me as if he'd never seen a woman without a veil.

"How much for the woman?" a tattered beanpole of a man asked Sean as he walked beside us later that night. He wasn't kidding. The hotel room was the only bit of space where we felt free from prying eyes and harassment.

Tangier was filled with scavengers, dirty children and men with few teeth and sketchy vision. Each dark corner seemed to hold secrets that daring travelers would feel compelled to discover. But there were only four days left of travel to reach our goal, Fez. We paid Mohammed 100 durum, about $10, and set off on our journey.

Settling into our train compartment, a portly, chatty man decided to join us. His name was also Mohammed. Pulling out a photo of his wife, he assured us, "I am not a polygamist, like so many of the men here," as if trying to gain our confidence. We shared more stories, and before long he invited us to join him in Asilah, an ancient Portuguese fishing town en route to Fez.

"There is a religious festival there this weekend," he said. "You can join us; go to *Hassams* (Moroccan baths,) get *henna* tattoos, eat with my family. Of course, you will need to buy *djellabas* (religious robes) to participate." Sean and I looked at each other with uncertainty, but it seemed too good to pass up.

At the Asilah train station he led us to his car and drove to an empty lot about a mile away, kicking up dust from decayed buildings. Barking dogs and curious children greeted us. "Everybody knows me here, I'm like Coca-Cola," he said, smiling confidently.

Mohammed Number 2 led us to a tiny, decrepit house where an insect-infested hole in the ground to our right served as the bathroom. "These flies are good luck," he said as he grabbed a broom and began attacking the insects covering a kitchen wall.

We put down our bags and before we could blink were whisked off by Mohammed to buy *djellabas*. We bargained a bit but still paid about 10 times too much for them. For some strange reason we trusted Mohammed and didn't want to let him down. He was our host, after all. After the purchases, Mohammed informed us that we'd have a few hours on our own to explore.

We headed for the mazelike, Arabic part of the city, the medina, which was set against the crashing ocean and had once been a thriving Portuguese port. It was supposed to be the most beautiful in Morocco.

The place was falling apart, but we couldn't deny its charm. Amid the decay were colorful street murals and eccentric boutiques filled with a hodge-podge of Moroccan wares.

As we walked along the ancient medina wall, a suspicious man with one eye watched us. "Psssssssst! PSSSSSSSSSSSSSSSSST!" he motioned to me as Sean wandered off to the ocean view. He walked up.

"Everybody here knows what is going on," he said. "You are being fooled. Ripped off. Don't follow Mohammed, he is only trying to take your money."

I yelled to Sean, grabbed his arm and rushed us away as I told him the story. "Oh my god," he said. "Everything is starting to make sense." We recounted the day's incidents. "There *isn't* a religious festival. The *djellabas* were a complete rip-off, the house is disgusting, we're being watched, we have no idea how to get out of this place," he continued. "AND, our passports are still at the house!" I added.

We sprinted back and banged on the door. A plump, stoic woman answered and let us in. Rushing over to our things we were relieved to find them intact. But Sean's anxious temperament made him paranoid. We still had two hours until Mohammed returned, and we had lost faith in his integrity. "I just want to get out of here," said Sean.

Pulling out a crumpled schedule, we discovered that the next train to Fez left at 1 a.m. We were stuck. When Mohammed finally returned, Sean launched at him. "You took our money, ripped us off, and there is no festival. Someone in town told us. We want our money back!" We had given him about $10 each, which all of a sudden seemed like a lot.

"Don't listen to what they tell you, the people here are just jealous," he said. "I can't give you your money because Farida has already started cooking for you. You can't leave the town until later, so you might as well relax and stay for a while."

We followed his advice, as much as possible. For dinner we were presented with *tagine* (a Moroccan dish of couscous and stewed meat and veggies) made with unidentifiable grisly meat and oily vegetables.

Hours passed, and finally it was time to go. We boarded a train full of sleeping, unkempt men and not a woman in sight. I huddled near Sean, and we tried our best to relax. The train was built around 1950, and nothing, including the plumbing, had been updated since then. Nature was calling, but the bathroom had no toilet paper and was full of indescribable filth. I weighed the options and returned to my seat.

Arriving in Fez at 3 a.m., we searched for a taxi. We flagged down a couple who were also looking. "I've never been so happy to see other Americans," I whispered to Sean as they approached. It turns out they were from California. The four of us managed to hail two cabs and spent the next hour and a half searching in vain for rooms. There was a conference going on, and they were all booked. Finally, our cabby pulled over and said, "If you want, you can all stay at my place." Under normal circumstances this would have been out of the question, but nothing about these circumstances was normal. We conversed with our compatriots quickly and decided to do it.

"Wow, this is amazing," we uttered as we entered what seemed like a Moroccan palace. Lush, embroidered cushions filled all corners of the huge, open room, and the bathroom featured a Western toilet complete with downy-soft toilet paper, to my delight.

We went to bed and were awakened in the morning by the smell of fresh mint tea and buttery pastries. The cab driver and his wife, an attractive and educated couple who spoke Arabic, French and English, had set up a succulent Moroccan spread. Freshly squeezed orange juice and piles of fresh strawberries, grapes and warm pastries were set before us. We couldn't believe their generosity.

We shouldn't have. After eating, our driver escorted us to the ATM. "Give me 500 durum (about $50) each." he demanded. Shocked, we did as we were told and were let off on the curb to fend for ourselves.

After this incident, we were determined to be independent, even if we were entirely out of our element and without a map to be found.

Venturing out into the blaring sun the next day from our hostel, we headed for the Fez medina, the largest in Morocco. "There is no map of it. Even the locals here don't know it by heart," we were warned. A taxi let us off and swarms of children surrounded us, throwing little stones and jeering as we approached.

The medina was like a medieval highway, filled with fast-paced old men steering iron egg carts, women decapitating chickens, children running to keep up with their mothers and the townsfolk bartering for deals. There would be no leisurely Sunday stroll.

"OW!!!" I exclaimed as an egg cart jammed into my leg. I jumped out of the way. "This is serious."

Sean and I explored as much as we could until we found ourselves lost in a Moroccan maze. Not sure how to escape, we both frantically searched for landmarks. "We passed this spice stand already, didn't we?" he asked. "It looks a whole lot like the other one," I replied. Children soon caught on to us and nagged us to be our guide. "I will lead you out of here," they said. "For 100 durum." Still feeling independent (or pigheaded, perhaps) we somehow managed to find our own way out.

Outside the maze we agreed that for once we desperately wanted to be somewhere not exotic. We headed to the *Ville Nouvelle* (New City) and ate *pomme frite* alongside tank-top clad Spaniards in a French café. A young boy about 8 approached us for money. "Go away!" Sean screamed at him. "I am going to *kill* you!" retorted the boy looking us square in the eyes.

After a brief jaunt to the nearby town of Meknes, where we were chased out of a cemetery by a group of Muslim women, we were ready to head home, or to any Western port for that matter. There were train and ferry delays along the way, but when we finally reached Spanish soil we both knelt to kiss the ground. It was a Sunday, and Algeciran families were coming out of church, dressed in their best. Old men and women sat outside on park benches reading the paper, and plazas had beautiful, functioning fountains. "This must be how Dorothy felt when she got back to Kansas," I said to Sean. He agreed. "Yeah. Maybe next time we should consult a travel guide," he replied.

A Journey to Tire a Man's Soul

by Don Sweet

"WHAT WAS THAT NOISE?" ASKED MY WIFE. "Just the kettle drum on the CD," I replied, only to look at my right side mirror and see bits of black material forming a wake behind us. We had blown a trailer tire.

My wife and I were traveling from Los Angeles to Lake Tahoe, towing our fifth-wheel trailer to a family reunion with our three grown children and their families. Highway 395 on the eastern edge of the Sierra Nevada was blessed by glorious weather. Now we could stop and enjoy the scenery as we waited for the Auto Club to replace our blown tire with a spare.

As soon as the spare tire was installed, we were back on the road. The next morning we stopped at a tire dealer in Bishop, bought our replacement and were on our way again. At Lake Tahoe, we were setting up camp when I noticed another tire was going flat. Taking it in for repair, I was advised the tread was separating. If these were defective, could the others be similarly flawed? Not taking any chances, we replaced all the tires.

The next day, walking back from the camp store to our site I noticed an unusual "shadow" on the roof of the trailer. The shadow turned out to be a four-foot dent caused by a tree branch at an RV Park in Reno. By now I was ready to turn in my Good Sam membership card. My wife suggested I go inside the trailer, lie down and try to think of something pleasant.

To cheer me up, our daughter recommended we take a trip around the lake via paddle wheeler. I agreed. It turned out this was a ruse to get me away from the campsite. They didn't want me to know that one of the new trailer tires had gone flat due to a faulty valve stem. The family wanted to get it fixed before I found out.

Strangers in the Night

by Karen Kutney

FOUR DAYS BEFORE DEPARTING FROM VANCOUVER for our honeymoon in Cuba, my husband, Joe, and I learned that our highly rated all-inclusive resort within walking distance of Varadero was overbooked. We, along with 40 others, had been rebooked by the tour company into a lower-class resort farther up the peninsula. Other travelers warned this would be a forced march. After much last-minute hassle, our travel agent found space at a third resort closer to town and half a star higher than the second choice establishment. In addition, the agent provided a "honeymoon bonus" plus a $50 refund.

Our flight stopped in Calgary, where we picked up several dozen teenagers headed to Cuba on a school band trip. They were all seated in our section, and while they were never truly impolite or intentionally obnoxious, their constant chatter and total inability to sit in the same seat longer than five minutes nearly drove me to violence by the end of the six-hour flight.

We arrived in Varadero just after 1 a.m. with 300 other arrivals, stripping off layers of clothing in a losing battle against the 95 percent humidity. During the long, long wait for our luggage, the band students maintained their exuberance, which made me hate them even more.

Finally, at 4 a.m., luggage in hand, we arrived at the resort. Our "honeymoon bonus" was two single beds, each with faded, dilapidated bedding, pushed together against a yellow, pockmarked wall.

"Well," Joe said, trying to brighten my mood, "we'll probably sleep better without each other's movement keeping us awake."

He was right, except for the fact that the beds were manufactured during the Mesozoic era. The mattresses were so worn that no matter where we slept, we inevitably rolled into a mangled heap in the center of each bed. Kissing goodnight meant clutching the inner edges of the beds, biceps bulging and lips straining to meet. The springs of my bed groaned like a wounded animal when I took a deep breath. While I prayed for exhaustion to overcome me, and daylight to bring a brighter perspective, Joe called from the bathroom to report that he had spotted a substantial, energetic bug.

The next morning we decided to explore our Caribbean retreat. Despite the socialist backdrop, the tourist scene in Cuba spurred as much conniving competition as mall parking at Christmas back home. Regardless of when you arrived at the beach, all of the lounge chairs were claimed. One couple told us that they noticed people sneaking around in the dark at midnight to stake their claim with towels for the following day. Joe and I were advised to bribe a hotel employee to hold a chair for us. Hard currency was preferred.

Mealtimes were another troubling matter. The "a la carte" restaurants (i.e. fine linens, service and food) required reservations that could only be made early in the morning on a first-come, first-served basis until the tables were filled. By sunrise, hordes of bleary-eyed people jammed the reservation table. Short of camping out in the lobby overnight like Who fans stalking concert tickets, we didn't have a chance of scoring a ticket.

That left the buffets. Here, space was nearly unlimited and the long hours of operation seemed to allow great flexibility. However, the tasty items were in short supply and only available for about the first 10 minutes after the doors opened. The buffet-wise relied on military strategies to beat out the rest of us. As neophytes, we watched in awe as entire families fanned out like running backs, making end runs around the slow-moving diners who insisted on knowing what they were about to eat. With the popular Cuban dishes disappearing in minutes, I decided to follow the experienced patrons who knowingly chose the best items, even if we couldn't tell what they were. The trick was to follow the most determined patrons and scoop copious quantities of mystery meat onto our plates before it all vanished. Joe's main duty was the meat and seafood section; I was responsible for desserts. Within a short time, we were a ballet of synchronized efficiency, and other newcomers chased us around the tables.

Late in the evening, tired from our learning curves, we returned to the lobby and the 24-hour "coffee and snack bar." The snack menu actually consisted of only one item: pencil-thin ham and cheese sandwiches that had strong metallic overtones from a cast-iron grill. These were also in limited supply, not because they were much good but because they were the only food available when the restaurants and buffets were closed. At least the coffee was excellent and the atmosphere lovely; the lobby was arranged in small groups of deeply padded wicker couches scattered amidst palms, hanging greenery and small pools and waterfalls. Joe and I happily spent an hour sipping espressos, nibbling on iron sandwiches and people watching. My husband and I briefly considered spending the night there, figuring that we stood a better chance of a good night's sleep than in our sinkhole beds upstairs.

Back in our room, Joe got reacquainted with the large, bug-like bathroom creature, which, fortunately for me, had misogynist tendencies and never appeared when I showed up. We rolled into our respective mangled heaps and turned out the lights. Within minutes, both of us were itching terribly.

"Do you think there are bugs in the beds?" Joe asked in a worried tone.

I shrugged in confusion while scratching my legs and toying with the idea of sleeping on the floor with a blanket from the closet. Finally, with no other option, we crawled back into bed.

Epilogue: The strangers in the night left us with multiple welts. After discovering that the lovely lobby pools and waterfalls were home to swarms of mosquitoes, we fled to Havana. Our original Varadero resort choice turned out to be available for the following week. The room and bed (a sturdy queen) were far superior, the lobby wildlife didn't nibble at us, and as far as we know, the bathroom was not bugged. The only things we missed were the iron sandwiches. Funny what honeymoons do to your taste buds.

Hannah's Horrible Holiday

by Hannah Ruth Davis, age 9

THANKSGIVING IS ONE OF THE BEST TIMES OF THE YEAR, right? Not for me . . . Well, most of it.

My family decided to take a trip from North Carolina to New Jersey by way of New York to see our relatives.

We took my dad's friend Doc along to see his family in New York City. Eager to see the Macy's Day Parade, we stayed at the apartment of Doc's mother. We took a big risk, because in the apartment above hers people were smashing cocaine into powder to sell to people who kept coming by. It kept us awake much of the night.

Doc's mom was so nice. She cooked the best rice and beans ever. One son was said to be an alcoholic, and we were warned not to wake him up when we first got there. Doc said he was wild like an animal! We were wall-to-wall Davises sleeping on the living room floor. It was crowded but worked OK.

The next morning, Doc cooked us up a big breakfast with another one of his brothers, Herman, who looked, and acted, like a cute, tough guy on TV's "Police Story." Then we walked to the Macy's parade. It was fun, but we could only see the balloons and the heads of people. The dinosaur got caught on a tree limb and popped open. A drunk "disco" man, dressed in shiny clothes, acted as if he were about to kiss me. Argg! He wanted attention and got too much.

Next we went to visit Doc's brother Ray and his wife at

their apartment on the old Polo Grounds. Just a week earlier a couple living one floor down had been murdered. Instead of worrying about the neighborhood, we all danced to Latin music played by Ray's family.

On Thanksgiving, the entire family dined on pizza. A day later we gathered at my Aunt Susie's house for our real holiday meal with 21 relatives. But when Aunt Susie opened the oven, none of the turkeys were done. We ate the rest of the meal while my mother read poems about everybody in our family. One of my cousins is 27 and is in Hollywood, trying to be a star. My Great Aunt Helen said that he hasn't worked a day in his life. He was there and my mother read this:

> "Handsome Robert
> Comes from afar
> From Hollywood
> A potential star.
> The Kato Kaelin
> Of our family
> And is just as cute
> Don't you agree?
> So spiritually minded
> He's no earthly good
> He needs to work
> Like every man should!"

On the way back to North Carolina, my dad was ticketed for speeding by a mean turnpike trooper. He called my dad a "liar" and told Doc to "shut up."

Back home, there had been a break-in. Someone had stolen $90 from my room. So much for Thanksgiving. Maybe Christmas will be better.

Good Morning, Yantai!

by John D. McCafferty

YOU CAN HAVE A FINE TIME TRAVELING AROUND CHINA without the help of a tour group, but be advised: Without speaking or writing Chinese, it can be very difficult, fatiguing, baffling, even a little frightening, particularly when you're trying to get some sleep. To understand what I'm talking about, why not join my wife, Sharon, and I on our summer ferry trip to Yantai.

Humming and grinding across the mouth of the Korea Bay out of Dalian, we finally drifted off to sleep after practicing English with two friendly but maddeningly persistent Chinese throughout a long evening in a sweaty, windowless stateroom.

At 2:32 a.m. blaring music from the speakers turned out to be our wakeup call. The ship was three hours early.

Soon a gaggle of Chinese and two confused Americans were shuffling wearily along the halls. Suddenly the two of us were in the cool night air, headed down the gangway to Yantai. At 3:30 a.m. we stood outside an official-looking building, the naked bulb of a dim parking lot lamp swaying gently in the sea breeze across the street. A smiling vendor with a cart and table was making tea and noodle soup for breakfast.

One of the piles on his table appeared to be liver. I hate liver, and it killed my appetite for soup. Sharon felt the

same way. Liver soup and noodles for breakfast at 4 a.m.?
I asked for two cups of tea, paid a pittance and sat on the
curb, a little discouraged.

The tea was nearly tasteless, even with sugar, which we
luckily had in our backpacks. Silence. Slurp. More silence.
Curbs are hard in any language. Sharon suggested that she
now understood why the acronym for flexible independent
travel was FIT.

Out of the darkness a guy pulled up in a motorized
pedicab, sort of a motorbike with just room for two in
the box-like cab. We showed him our guidebook that had
the Chinese characters for the "guesthouse" that was our
destination. He puzzled over these for quite a while, finally
nodding and motioning for us to climb in. I wasn't worried, even if he did come to a stop from time to time and
look all around.

After driving in very large circles for 15 minutes, he
stopped in a lighted intersection and pointed to the rear
of a building. After the driver left we realized this was not
our hotel. Unable to locate our destination, Sharon and I
discovered a tattered neighborhood pool table, a popular
form of outdoor recreation. Both of us jumped on the felt
surface, stretched out and closed our eyes. Sharon was able
to rest but I couldn't get comfortable. We talked a little
and I kept banging the tabletop with my elbows and knees.
Suddenly there was a loud knocking from underneath!
We had a tablemate down on the ground below us. All he
wanted was a little courtesy.

Overhead, a single naked light bulb, swaying in the
breeze, illuminated the neighborhood. The temperature
was nearly perfect, like summer nights at our California
home on the Pacific. We dozed. Looked around. Dozed.

When I woke at dawn, a senior citizen, swinging his arms in a morning exercise routine, strode by across the street. As I was easing myself off the pool table to take a look around, a woman rode up on her pedicab, pulling a portable fast food stand resembling a big popcorn machine.

Behind her was the night soil man towing a brown tank behind his bicycle. He stopped about 20 yards to our right, across the street, and carried a long pooper-scooper to the wall of an apartment building. He opened a trap door near the base of the building, inserted the scoop and withdrew the sewage. He made two more trips, mounted his carriage and rode on. The smell followed him away, and we could breathe again.

After breakfasting with one of the street vendors, we headed off, leaving our bunkmate sleeping peacefully beneath the pool table. We found our hotel in seconds.

Because it was right around the corner.

Lost in Baja

by Russ Faure-Brac

I WAS ON AN EIGHT-DAY SPRING ADVENTURE with my 23-year-old son Gabe, kayaking on the Sea of Cortez and driving back to California up the Pacific Coast. The two of us drove a 1992 Toyota pickup with a camper shell, two Ocean Kayaks mounted on a rack, and thought we were prepared for anything.

On day 6 we drove north, seeking Mission San Antonio and hotrodding on poor dirt roads as we wended our way. Very unexpectedly, Gabe and I encountered a tall dirt berm blocking the road. There was no way around it. Our map, which showed a double dotted line through here, had led us astray. A local rancher assured us that another road further north led to Highway 1.

More hotrodding, boy are we having fun, gee look at all that water on the road up ahead, I better drive on the side where the ground looks firmer. It wasn't. Three of our four wheels sank up to their axles in the gooey mud. The two of us spent the next eight hours digging and jacking up the truck to put rocks under the tires for better traction. It didn't work.

At 5 p.m. we gave up for the day and talked about our plight over a campfire. There was no hope of anybody driving by—our location was just too remote. If necessary, we could pack food and water and hike 40 miles to where

160

we might find people. Another possibility was to drag the kayaks half a mile to the beach and paddle down the coast in search of helpful fishermen. It would have helped if either of us knew where we were.

Covered in mud I slept fitfully. Saturday dawned. April 1. A cruel joke. The thought of crawling on my belly under the truck again was appalling. Gabe had the brilliant suggestion that we hike up a hill and look around. That put us high enough to see a fishing boat just off our beach. We yelled our heads off and chased them down. They were anchored in a cove ready to abalone dive. Gabe yelled, *"Pagamos para ayuda,"* which translates loosely as "We pay dinero if you save our butts."

The three fishermen were gracious, but the looks on their faces said, "Only idiots get their trucks stuck in the mud. Why were you driving in the mud in the first place?" The head guy, Trini, offered to boat back to Punta Blanca and return with his truck to pull us out. As they had to forego a full day of abalone diving he wanted $100 for their services. Given our situation it sounded like a bargain. A burly character named Jose stayed with us as the other two left. About two hours later Trini returned.

After two broken ropes and eight pulls they finally freed our Toyota. Trini brought out Coca-Cola and brandy to celebrate, and everyone drank a toast. But he also said that his two friends needed to be paid. We had thought the $100 was full payment, but weren't going to argue. Since we had almost no money left, we offered each of them a piece of our diving gear. Unfortunately, Gabe kept offering them more and more equipment until my diving gear duffel was significantly lightened. He even gave away his watch. Gabe used to be a waiter and believes in tipping well.

When it was time to go, Trini explained that we were at a beach called Huatamote, which I believe is not marked on any map in existence. To reach Highway 1, he said, disregard the roads shown on our maps and take the route that he drew for us.

We left the three fishermen at 1:15 p.m. When we reached a river crossing at Rio San Jose, I had the feeling we had discovered a death trap. Reeds growing on the riverbanks reminded me of the quicksand in the old movies I watched as a kid. Gabe and I backtracked to another road going west and then north to San Jose Fish Camp. I thought our troubles were over. Friendly fishermen pointed north and said, "Take this road." It is *muy grande* all the way to Catavina on Highway 1—the proverbial "you can't miss it."

After miles of bumpy dirt roads, Gabe noticed the tailgate had opened from the constant pounding. Our spare gas can and other items had fallen out. Backtracking led us to the trail of our droppings—an ammo can, a tub of whipped butter and, thank goodness, the gas can. Heading north again, every road we tried petered out. In great frustration, we schlepped back to the fish camp (by now we knew the way to San Jose) and offered to pay them if they would lead us out. We pulled out $6.50, our last remaining American money. They didn't think it was much but they took pity on these helpless, mud-covered gringos.

It was now about 5 p.m. Our guides took an immediate right turn from the camp (we had gone straight earlier) and led us to the road. After about two miles they waived us on and returned to camp. We had one more river crossing to negotiate, which we reached at dusk. The 200-foot crossing was about two feet deep. Gabe closed his eyes and prayed all the way.

We continued driving in the dark as the bumps battered our truck. An hour later I heard a screech. The camper shell had slipped off its clamps and was falling off the truck. Gabe and I took the kayaks off, reclamped the shell, reloaded the boats and headed on our merry way. After several more bumpy hours, Highway 1 appeared out of nowhere. A six-mile drive south led to Catavina and gas paid for with the last of our last traveler's check. At 10 p.m. we began the forbidden—driving Highway 1 at night. Potholes, narrow lanes, non-existent shoulders and free-roaming cattle and horses make this road hazardous even during the day. Our journey ended in Ensenada at 3 a.m. I took over driving to Tijuana and we arrived at dawn on Sunday.

You know those bad dreams where everything keeps going wrong? Within a half-mile of the border red lights flashed in my rear view mirror. The Tijuana cop insisted I had been speeding. Looking at my license, he pointed out it had expired a month ago. He said I had to pay a 4,500-peso fine to him, in cash, of course. That's roughly $600. I had 22 pesos left. Could he take a check? No. Could he take a MasterCard? No. He had us follow him to a bank so I could withdraw pesos from an ATM. I tried to make the Spanish-speaking thing work but failed. Terrifying images of being tossed into a Mexican jail ran through my head. Taking a deep breath, I went to the cop's car to explain. Shaking his head in disbelief, he gave up, uttering something like "Get your ass out of here."

I jumped in the truck, and Gabe drove across the border. Our troubles were over. Interstate 5 was great until the front end of the truck started vibrating like a jackhammer.

All we needed was a $500 front-end alignment and brake repair.

Dried Fish & Impulsive Love

by Lisa Alpine

As I sat in a coffeehouse in Bogota, sharp pieces of dried fish that clung to my cotton trousers were scratchy and annoying. The hard plastic chair—a neon shade of Orange Julius— pressed the bits deeper into my flesh. I squirmed with discomfort. Boyfriend Scott didn't look a whole lot better sitting across from me.

Usually I traveled alone on my import/export journeys when I collected unusual artifacts for my two retail stores in California. Puddle-jumping on prop planes from Bogota into the heart of the Amazon Basin to Leticia is not for those who like first-class comforts. Staph-infected bites and scars on my arms and leg from mosquitos after every trip south were merit badges to me, evidence of survival and adventure. Malaria, piranha, drug lords, lecherous men, I always came back to California in one piece—well, almost.

So what was I doing bringing a boyfriend with me on this trip? Scott hated the jungle and the Indians I traded with, couldn't paddle a canoe or take a photograph. He was in a constant state of hysteria no matter how glorious the gigantic Victoria Reina lillypads or how strange and mythical the pink river dolphins.

How ironic in a way since I'm Scandinavian-blonde and delicate in appearance, while he, Scott Duncan, is a swarthy mix of Chinese and Scotch.

So this nasty, whiny, jet-black-haired boyfriend and I fled back up to cool, refreshing Bogota in a cargo plane. We perched atop planks of stinky fish in an unpressurized cabin. Scott quacked so loud I could hear his complaints over the propeller's incessant bronchial roar.

The pilot forced us to get out on the runway when we landed. We had to jump out as the plane was taxiing. He was not supposed to have passengers. We scrambled across the tarmac, hopped a chain link fence and flagged down a bus to town. We were so stinky there was no problem getting a seat as the passengers gave us lots of room.

So here we sat, together, over a cup of Colombian coffee in a modern plastic cafeteria. Scott, whom I wanted to push out of the airplane at high altitude less than an hour ago, suddenly looked delicious, a song in his eyes as he felt my light touch. His slightly torn plaid shirt hung off broad shoulders.

Suddenly, I wanted to marry this man. This Scott Duncan man. This horse trainer from home whom I met at a dude ranch and didn't even like at first.

He read my mind and proposed over the tiny cup of café negro. Was it the dizzying effect of the fish smell, perhaps an aphrodisiac that only we had just discovered? Had we stumbled upon the "smell of love?"

Whatever vapor caused us to impulsively commit to spending the rest of our days together in marital bliss only lasted long enough for me to write a rosy letter about our future to my parents.

My poor parents. A daughter roaming the world to places they wouldn't dream of traveling to and she by herself. Finally, a man to take care of her! Two weeks later when we arrived back in California, they were waiting for us at the terminal gate with a dozen red roses and a bottle of champagne.

My father, ever the Old World charmer, "Come, let's celebrate this joyful news of your marriage."

"What are you talking about?"

My parents nodded and smiled knowingly at Scott with a look that said, "Now you get to deal with her whimsical, fickle nature."

The letter. I had forgotten about the proclamation of love I had written about to them in that far away coffee-house in Bogota. The smell of the dried fish suddenly filled my nostrils and I remembered the proposal that wore off within a day of delivery. Quicker than the fish smell and with less of a trace.

Pursuing the Mists of Ambon

by Sunny Lucia

DESCRIBING JAKARTA MAKES ME WANT TO HOLD UP MY HANDS and start enumerating reasons to skip this bustling Far East capital. It is a hot, humid, confusing labyrinth of unmarked streets. The city presents a raw edge that increased our ordinary attitude of caution, which was heightened by the overwhelming presence of heavily armed police and military personnel. Jakarta's tourist chicanery is also dreadful. Our encounters with persistent opportunism came directly out of the "special cautions" section of our travel book. We experienced several popular tourist scams here: 1) the "officially licensed government tour guide" on his day off; 2) the guide who offered to take us into the inner, "forbidden" section of the Great Mosque; and 3) the rogue who read museum exhibit explanations printed in English aloud to us and then insisted on a guide fee.

The banks were another example of Jakarta's attempt to confound and control. I found a profusion of banks in this city and a wide divergence of governing rules. The exchange rate was volatile, and when the rate was more favorable to the rupiah we were able to cash traveler's checks relatively easily. When the rate reflected a stronger U.S. dollar, the banks placed an immediate limit on the amount of cash available to a person daily, raised their service fees and reduced their exchange hours. When I wanted to purchase tickets for a Pelni ship to travel through the archipelago and needed $800 cash, I had to go to three banks to get the money. Spending an entire morning cashing six traveler's checks was a bit of a nuisance, but this struggling economy allowed us to purchase a high level of luxury on what my husband, Steve, and I considered a very frugal budget: $800 purchased first-class accommodations and meals for both of us for 14 days.

Our planned adventure was inspired by Somerset Maugham's steamship trips through Indonesia in the 1920s. He savored the verdant landscapes and exotic indigenous tribes of the most geographically dispersed island nation in the world. His trip could be loosely replicated by booking passage on a Pelni ship, the only public trans-island transportation available. In his youth, Steve had read a book titled *The 10,000 Things* and was enamored with the thought of seeing the mists surrounding the port of Ambon.

On our first morning in the city, we grabbed our Jakarta map and asked our hotel owner to circle the location for the Pelni office. Our English translation map was creatively scaled and seduced us into thinking that the walk would be short. Two and a half dusty and emission-choked hours later, we approached an opening in a block-long barbed wire fence and explained to armed guards that we wanted to buy tickets to Ambon; three of them escorted us to the entrance of a 10-story, red brick building.

Pelni operated 16 cargo freighters from Medan in the west to Jayapura in the east of the archipelago. The smallest ships housed 969 beds; the largest offered 2,000 with air conditioning, meals, dining rooms and private cabins. When we headed to the jam-packed first floor ticket room to get in line, six heavily armed security personnel immediately surrounded us. The only English-speaking guard abruptly commanded us to go to the second floor, insisting we could only book first- or second-class passage.

The second floor appeared vacant, but an English-speaking Muslim woman tried to help us. Gradually a dozen women, all in full hijab dress, gathered around to watch the entertainment. After an hour of giggling, pointing and more passing spectators, our new friend finally explained that we were at the wrong building. "You have to go to the main office. Go see Captain Hilliard on floor 5."

We waited an hour on the fifth floor before Captain Hilliard, the managing director of Pelni, emerged from his office. After our now oft-repeated explanation he said, "Oh, yes we can do that here, but it will take time to get you the same cabin through the whole journey." After several hours, Captain Hilliard finally wrote out a ticket for our second choice, the Kerinci, from TG Priok (Jakarta) to Ambon in the Spice Islands, returning 14 days later to the town of Surabaya on Java. He told us to return with cash the next day. "And, be careful on the ship," Captain Hilliard added. We expressed our gratitude with "Terima kasih" and practically skipped to the elevator, elated with our accomplishment.

I never asked why our first choice, the Rinjani with 2,000 beds and three decks of economy passage, was completely booked.

At first, our ship was pure luxury. We had a first-class cabin with the comfort of a private bathroom after more than a month of youth hostels. Doting waiters served three meals a day in a first-class dining room. We passed time leaning over the railing watching schools of dolphins, barracuda, stingray and flying fish skim alongside the ship against a backdrop of hundreds of romantic islands.

The spotless vessel boasted wide polished teak promenades on seven decks and a scarcity of benches that puzzled us until we witnessed the people who eventually boarded. As we walked around the first day, we knew that all 1,800 beds and bunks were full and saw about 600 people scattered on the decks sleeping on mats. At Surabaya, the first port, 1,000 more passengers boarded. At the next evening stop in Makassar, crushing crowds exited and entered the boat for hours. By our third day, every deck, stairwell and hallway was tightly packed with people arranged like human jigsaw puzzles—at least 4,000 in all by now. Opening the door to leave our cabin meant displacing 10 people. Strolls on the deck turned into acrobatics as we tried to step on as few toes as possible: "Pardon me, excuse me, I'm sorry, hello, good morning."

Many passengers were surprised to see us; by evening word had spread that we were Americans, not Dutch. People followed us, wanting to feel our skin or asking us to touch a baby. Sometimes groups would surround us to ask questions. The first was always, "Do you have children?" When we said yes, giving their ages (26 and 25), the next question was always, "Why are they not with you?" Indonesian families travel together, even when the children are grown.

We learned that the boat was crowded because of the festival month of Lebaron, which follows the Islamic holy month of fasting called Ramadan. During Lebaron, family units traditionally travel to the oldest relatives' home. Coupled with this, for the first time in 30 years Chinese New Year overlapped Lebaron. All of Southeast Asia was on the move.

With a continuing stream of self-appointed translators, we learned more from our fellow passengers about Indonesian culture (including such random tidbits as how cloves were grown in Sumatra) while carefully sidestepping questions about war-torn East Timor. Passengers had warned us to be careful of government "spies" because they were known to trap people into making conversational blunders. During our voyage several Sumatrans were escorted off the ship at gunpoint.

Dozens of passengers thrust their cameras at us each day, asking if they could take a picture with us. I was touched by the gentle, sincere, inquisitive nature of the Indonesian people. As I smiled and said hello, played peek-a-boo with infants and exchanged high-fives with the older kids, the psychic fear of the crowd faded.

And the sights along the way to Ambon were amazing. Each port offered different and incredible scenes, not the least of which was the docking process. The instant the stairway platform was secured to the dock, hundreds of yellow-jacketed boys climbed over the railings and forged through the huddled masses hunting for bags and packages to carry for tips. The sweating, shoving, packed mob of people was frightening. It could take 30 to 45 minutes to move from the lobby through the doors down the gangplank and onto the dock. Slipping or falling meant certain injury. We loved joining our fellow passengers on trips into port towns during the three-to-six-hour stops, always carefully confirming the ship's departure time. If we returned too late, it would be nearly a month before another ship would arrive

Most of the port towns were quiet places with painted flower-box homes and white picket fences. Old forts from foreign occupation days were now parks and playgrounds. The residents, like our fellow ship passengers, were shy, yet curious about foreigners. Teenagers would wave to us with "Hello Misters," while younger children hid behind their mothers.

After six days of oppressive heat, we sailed through the fog to our destination. The mists of Ambon shrouded the gate to the Spice Islands as our ship gently nosed its way forward. Iris, one of the young women we had met on the boat, lived in Ambon and walked with us into town. A group of high school students surrounded us en masse and chatted non-stop about American music and shopping centers as they happily escorted us back to the dock.

At our dusk departure from Ambon, a city troubled by inter-religious tensions, security was extraordinary. Machine-gun armed militia lined the seventh deck railing about 20 feet apart, guns at ready aimed toward the boarding area. More police lined the dock and port entrance; they searched many of the bundles being carried on board. Ticket checks were more thorough, coming and going more difficult. The locals remained undisturbed and amiable about life in a police state.

I was impressed by the Indonesians' ability to get along. Although every last inch of space was claimed on the boat deck, we saw no fights, loud arguments or territorial squabbles. Children did not demand and scream. Parents didn't yell, and we heard no scolding, saw no spanking. Even when it rained, soaking deck passengers and their belongings, there was no tumult, no shouting. Their patience and sense of dignity made me realize that these gentle people knew the true meaning of safe travel. They understood the importance of respecting their fellow passengers. Here the golden rule really did apply. It was a pleasure to share their journey.

Stabbed and Gouged

by Joe Kempkes

WHEN I WAS STABBED DURING A ROBBERY ATTEMPT on a visit to Buyukada, an idyllic island off the Turkish coast, I thought my trip had bottomed out. I was wrong. Running from my assailant, I spotted a gardener in a small pickup truck. He took me to a first aid station where they called the Turkish Coast Guard. With help from two men, I staggered to the dock and was loaded aboard a coast guard cutter, which sped me to Istanbul.

When we arrived, an officer flagged down a battered truck carrying two men and spoke to them. They put me into the truck and calmly drove toward the downtown.

The driver stopped for gas and asked me for money. I hadn't changed my traveler's checks yet into Turkish lira so I gave him the few dollars I had on me. We drove on. He pulled over again and started talking to some people. I thought he might be asking for directions to the hospital, but he went into a store and came out drinking a beer and started joking with the other guy in the truck. I jumped out of the truck gurgling blood, bent over from the waist and started running—where to, I wasn't sure. They came running after me and threw me into the truck and drove away.

They took me to a large brick Kafkaesque-looking 18th-century armory. At the door my new friend turned me over to someone who took my bag and passport and flopped me down on an old Army cot.

A few hours later, a young woman pushed a metal cart loaded with food into the ward. If you wanted food, you had to pay for it. Naturally, she refused to accept my traveler's checks. When I asked her for water she pointed to a drinking fountain. I pressed the button, but nothing came out. I never did find out where the toilet was, assuming there was one (probably a pay toilet, anyway).

During the night, car crash victims were brought in and flopped down on cots. They had broken limbs and screamed in agony. I was later told that this was the "poor people's hospital," the place where people went to die.

I was bleeding internally from my upper back wound and had to rise up from the cot to get air into my one working lung. I was sure that if I fell asleep, I would never wake up. Sometime during the night, I passed out from exhaustion and blood loss and subsequently woke up looking at two well-dressed Turkish men, who had been sent by the American Consulate. Before letting me into their late-model Chevy, they asked for money. My hands were covered with blood, so they pulled my traveler's checks out of my pocket and I signed over a $20 check.

Four blocks away was the Admiral Bristonzy Hospital—the "American" hospital. Five minutes after arrival I was on the operating table with a tube in my chest. My collapsed lung was pumped up, and they extracted about two pints of blood from my chest cavity.

The next day, the Istanbul Homicide Squad came in at lunchtime. After I had one bite of food, the inspector took the tray away and proceeded to grill me like I was the perpetrator rather than the victim. He brought in two suspects whom I couldn't possibly identify.

When I couldn't help the inspector, he became infuriated and loudly ordered a nurse's aide to take my lunch tray out of the room.

The following day, the detective showed up again with more suspects and I told them the same thing. I had trouble talking, and the trauma was making my body go numb. Two days later the pain came back in force. Without morphine I would have jumped out of the window.

I was in a double room with a patient who had a parade of loud visitors who chain smoked and were into horseplay, pushing each other into his bed and mine.

Televised Turkish soap operas and children's cartoons supplied the sound track.

On my eighth day there, it was time for a jailbreak.

I disengaged and tied off the tubes that ran into my forearm, grabbed by bag and went to the cashier's office. I paid my bill of 5,409 Turkish lira (about $700 at the time) reclaimed my passport and caught a bus to the airport. My doctor probably still wonders what happened to me.

When I arrived at Heathrow Airport in London, I was strip searched since I had lost 60 pounds during my travels in Afghanistan, India, Thailand and Nepal and looked like a zombie. When they started prying the heels off of my boots, I lifted up my shirt to show the bandages, which freaked them out. They rushed me through customs, and I caught a plane to Toronto, where my brother lives.

While I've had three other near-death experiences, it was this incident in Turkey that has most affected my trajectory, making me aware that while life has had its unexpected experiences, it's always been a precious gift.

Love in Sangriaville

by Alison James

A WEEK AT HOME in my cramped Manhattan apartment would have been more restful than my Caribbean vacation, but also a lot duller. It was the first trip I would ever take with the love of my life.

Tom and I arrived in San Juan, Puerto Rico, on a Saturday morning in early October. We planned to spend two days exploring the city and then take off for rural parts of the island in a rental car. Given how little time we would have in the cosmopolitan center, we had to make our first day count. Within an hour after our arrival, he and I found our hotel, dropped off our things and set out with our maps.

Our afternoon began with a leisurely stroll down Ponce de Leon Avenue in Old San Juan. The boulevard quickly gave way to a busier highway, lined by the ocean on one side, and office buildings on the other. The day was hot and the sun should have sent us looking for shade. Though parched and tired, we walked on taking in all the sites with the enthusiasm of first-day vacationers. When we arrived back at the hotel that evening, Tom and I were exhausted but satisfied with our first day of sightseeing.

After showering Tom came out of the bathroom with a look of horror on his face. As he walked into the light, I could see why. His shoulders, neck and arms were covered with enormous, yellow blisters. His legs and the tops of his feet were bright red and almost raw. By midnight he was shivering and could barely move and I spent the next 36 hours nursing him back to health, putting creams on his body and medical sprays on his chest, shoulders and face. The pain was even worse the second day and we had to sleep with pillows between us so I wouldn't accidentally touch him. If he did move his arms the wrong way he would cry out in agony. During those first two days, I witnessed Tom's less-than-glamorous side from every angle. I rubbed him down with therapeutic lotion, helped him shower and changed his clothes.

On Monday he was feeling somewhat better, and we set out again to explore. We planned to drive to El Yunque National Forest and walk along the rainforest trails. Since neither of us owned a car in Manhattan, we were excited about getting the rental and being able to travel all over. When we picked up the car, Tom asked me if I would drive because he was still feeling slightly ill. Then, he threw me a new curve ball. For the first time he told me about his recurring car crash nightmares. In these dreams he dies in a bloody highway wreck, crushed between metal and glass. My first question, "Am I in the car?" didn't make him feel better. Normally a confident man, Tom became a bunny in a cave inside an automobile. I drove.

We spent the day in the rainforest and hiked along the tropical trails. Toward dusk we were both hungry and tired so we set out to find a place to stay for the night off the highway. Although the island of Puerto Rico is flat along the shore, the center is a full-fledged mountain range with all the trimmings: winding roads, narrow passages, poorly lit sections, drop-offs with no guardrails, stray dogs galore and stringy, low-hanging vegetation. Add to those circumstances an unfamiliar rental car, road signs in Spanish, a driver who hasn't been behind the wheel in two years and a frightened, anxious, sunburned boyfriend in the passenger seat and you have a very long ride.

We didn't have an accident that night, but we did have one of the worst screaming matches of our dating career. During the rest of the week more challenges arose, usually while we were driving. Several times I wanted to open the door and push him over a cliff and yell, "Are you still afraid of crashes?"

I signed us up for horseback riding on our last night on the island, to fulfill my personal fantasy of "riding a stallion on the beach at sunset." I thought it would be a romantic way to end our Caribbean stay. Tom loves dogs and other animals, so I assumed he would adore horses, too. Wrong. Needless to say, I was taken aback when he kept repeating two words: "Christopher Reeve." He wasn't kidding around. He was, indeed, terrified of being thrown from a horse and winding up a paraplegic.

When he realized our two-hour ride was non-refundable, Tom reluctantly agreed to give it a shot. I rode Sonja, an old, obedient horse who liked to be at the front of the pack. Tom rode a horse called Sangria. Because Tom's horse liked to go off the trail, we were separated for most of the ride. I would glance back and see him bounding over hills. His eyes were always wide and occasionally he was laughing. I was thrilled to see that he was having fun. Halfway through the ride, our guide informed me that Sangria "bounces" more than most. I wasn't sure what she meant until we arrived back at the stable. Tom's smile during our trek was, in fact, forced. His hands were covered with blisters from what he later described as his "death grip" on the reigns. His pants were ripped up the middle and both sides of his legs hurt because the saddle chafed his sunburned skin. I spent the rest of the night caring for my phobic, injured, exhausted, blistered, sunburned boyfriend.

Okay, I learned that Tom's not perfect. Neither am I. But we survived our first trip together, had fun and have since gotten engaged. Needless to say, we won't be doing much horseback riding on our honeymoon.

Not So Royale Isle

by Charlie Finley

THE SIX OF US WERE FRIENDS, members of the same church in Richmond, Virginia, who had vacationed for the first time together two years before in Maine. We'd enjoyed a two-week trek on the Allagash Whitewater Wilderness, paddling some 145 miles during a 10-day period and camping at a new spot along the way each night. So we decided to go on vacation together again. One of us suggested Isle Royale, a national park in the northwest corner of Lake Superior, about 30 miles off Thunder Bay, Canada. The only way to get there is by ferry from Michigan's upper peninsula or from Grand Portage, Minnesota. It is a haven for kayakers, bikers, photographers, backpackers, moose and fishermen. There are no roads on the island, and don't even think about using your cell phone. All visitors are briefed on wilderness etiquette on the islands laced with 165 miles of trails. You haul out all of your trash, leave only footprints, pick no flowers, burn your used toilet paper and take your cigarette butts with you. Isle Royale hosts 15,000 to 18,000 guests a year, less than the traffic at Yellowstone National Park on any summer weekend. But Isle Royale's claim to fame is its first place ranking of repeat visitors for any national park in the U.S. system, an amazing tribute considering how hard it is to get there.

In November 2001, on a cold fall evening, the six of

us—Paul and Linn Kreckman, Len and Rachel Cobb and my wife, Brenda, and I—gathered for dinner in our living room with maps and visions of a great vacation. We were not deterred by the guidebook mentioning seasickness on the four-hour Lake Superior ferry ride from Michigan. Or warnings to take plenty of insect spray with maximum DEET to deflect the black flies, mosquitoes and other wee beasties. Or that the eggs of a tapeworm could not be eliminated through the usual hand-operated water filters. The best course was to boil all your drinking water for at least three minutes. We decided to bring along three gallons of Coleman fuel for this task. Our plans called for us to be dropped off with all our gear and three canoes at a point midway down the island. Then, through a series of portages from one interior lake to another, we would make our way back over the following eight days to the departure point for the ferry back to Copper Harbor, Michigan. The park rangers were very deliberate about wanting to know our intended itinerary, "just in case," and we filed our hiking and canoeing plan with them. I should mention that our ages ranged from 49 to 61, and most of us had desk jobs back in Richmond. I don't know that any of us actually "worked out" to get ready for the trip. While mapping our final itinerary about a month before the 1,600-mile road trip from Richmond, none of us translated the word "portage" into something that meant tortuous, dangerous, slippery and grueling, requiring Indiana Jones-like stamina. The trails between the interior lakes were only roots and rock without markers. None of these slippery slopes had clear routes for canoe careening. The notation on the Isle Royale map indicating a .6-mile portage from one lake to another didn't really translate

181

into actually carrying all 215 pounds of gear, plus our 85-pound canoe. I don't know what we were thinking, but I can tell you that neither the guidebooks, nor the park information, nor the Internet gave us a feel for the portages.

On our first night in the campground, I stepped out of my tent and noticed it was really beginning to rain. We had had rain off and on, but this was RAIN. Not only rain, but rain accompanied by tremendous noise, sort of like Niagara Falls in the distance. What could that noise be? All six of us were awake at this point, stacking gear vertically, trying to avoid the paths of the water rushing under our tent floors. Of course, the important things to keep dry are your clothes, sleeping bags, matches, food, medical supplies, etc. If you've ever camped, you know what a scramble it is when in the dark of the night it starts to pour. Obviously, sleeping was over for the night, and we sopped up and shifted gear around until about 10:30 a.m. when the waters of Noah finally moved on. Then the wind began. Two days later I met a hiker who brought everyone up to date on the storm that had hit Isle Royale. There had been winds of 62 miles per hour and 16-foot waves around the edges of the island. That must have been the distant noise we heard, the waves hitting the rocky edges of the shore. The storm had prevented the ferry from making its run from Minnesota for the first time in 32 years. The portages got worse as we ticked off the days. The first one was a mere .4 mile; the second was .6 mile. We did two lakes and two portages that day in order to keep moving and stay on schedule. Each portage took four trips back and forth from lake to lake. Although we had waterproof maps and two GPS devices, I found it nearly impossible to see the portage trail marker signs at the lake's end. It was a

4-inch square post, maybe 3 feet tall, painted brown with a 3-inch tall letter "P" marking the trailhead.

Our first trip on this portage took just under an hour, but that included unloading the canoe and getting all the gear up on land. The weather was warm, about 75 degrees, and all we needed was a T-shirt to keep the bugs at bay. Our group found a dry place to camp, sunshine and enjoy several restful days before it was time to move to a new campsite. This gave us time to catch up in our journals, read those books we'd brought along, do some fishing, take a nap and possibly finish writing our wills.

By Monday night we were all rested and dreading the last 2.5-mile portage. On Tuesday it took the six of us all day to portage two of the three canoes and our gear over a very rugged trail to Moskey Basin. About 7 p.m. we ran out of daylight and energy and waited until the next day to pick up the third canoe. Of course we avoided the shelter with the hornet's nest that had been roped off by the rangers with warning signs and yellow "caution" tape. Dinner that night was canned ham, instant potatoes, fruit, beans and Tang.

Later, back in my office in Richmond, I realized we did have a good time, in spite of the mosquitoes, the rain, the storm, the portages and a couple of nights spent napping on wet sleeping bags. None of us became seasick on the ferry, and no one dumped their canoe, broke a leg, lost a credit card or was gored by a moose. Our little venture reminded me of a quote from Mark Twain: "I'm glad I did it, partly because it was well worth doing, but chiefly because I shall never have to do it again."

The Baboon

by Diane Carlson

SHOULD YOU EVER BE DRIVING AND ENCOUNTER A BABOON, if you have even the *slightest* inkling that the baboon has been fed by humans make sure your windows are rolled up.

My 5-year-old daughter, Zoe, and I were spending three months in South Africa while I was doing research. My sister Charlotte joined us for the last two weeks of our stay, and the three of us rented a car and headed east to Kruger National Park for a few days. We were looking forward to seeing giraffes, elephants, lions, hippos and especially cheetahs, for Zoe. I was also looking forward to driving on the left side of the road. Everything in the car was reversed, and I was focused on not indicating a left turn by accidentally flipping on the windshield wipers.

At the end of our first day we were speeding back to our camp before the gates were locked for the night. We slowed down when we saw several cars had stopped to look at a handful of baboons on the side of the road. We eased past them, stopped for a moment to take a picture, then sped on and made it back to our camp just in time.

The next morning, the baboons were in the same place we'd seen them the day before. This time we stopped to watch. No other people were around. We were thrilled when one of the females ambled across the road right in

front us and turned to parallel the car on the other side of
the road. I got a great picture and put the camera down
just as she began to approach the car.

Before I knew it, she had hopped up into the window
and was sitting in the frame. Charlotte and I found this hilarious, but my daughter didn't. In the seat next to me, Zoe
began to scream. Charlotte opened a map and hung it like
a curtain between her and the baboon to keep the baboon
from coming in any further.

The baboon did not act aggressively and seemed entirely unimpressed by our caterwauling. As further evidence
of her disrespect, she snatched up our plastic bag of trash
and leapt right back out the window and up on to our roof
with it.

Even with the windows now up, Zoe was yelling.

Meanwhile, an enormous male from the group had
taken the bag from the curious female and sat down by
the rear of the car inspecting the loot. We couldn't see him
too well back there, but we could see quite easily the tri-
umphant female as she came down and sat on the hood.
Apparently we were more interesting now.

She looked at us, we at her. I continued to assure Zoe
that the baboons couldn't get in the car. Charlotte and I still
giggled. I took pictures of the baboon as she came closer to
sit on my sideview mirror and look in at us. When the male
was finished shredding the bag and most of its contents
and had flung them here and there, all of the baboons took
off into the brush. We couldn't see them but didn't want to
assume they couldn't see us.

As much as we wanted to be on our way, our environmental consciences couldn't leave the shredded trash there
on the road. I started the car and like a really bad parallel

parking job maneuvered the car back and forth around the trash so that Charlotte would only have to open her car door an inch or so to slip her hand out and pick up the pieces off the ground.

The Urge to Merge

by Brenda McGee

IT WAS THE SECOND DAY OF OUR SIX-DAY TRIP. We had spent the previous night in Logansport, Indiana, and drove 90 miles this sunny Thursday morning to have breakfast in Lafayette. We held hands through breakfast, enjoying the approach of our fifth wedding anniversary that we hoped to celebrate atop the Gateway Arch in St. Louis.

Since we had taken two-lane roads most of the trip and needed to make up some time, we decided to get on the interstate.

Three semis blocked the lane I was trying to merge into; they had no room to move over for me.

In a split second, the merge lane rounded a blind curve, and to my surprise, a white state highway truck was parked in my lane. The workers were pulling shovels from the tailgate, and one chubby worker looked startled to see my van approaching their pick-up. He began to run clumsily along the side of the truck disappearing from view in front of it.

I shrieked, "What shall I do?"

My husband, Thomas, yelled, "Take the ditch!"

I turned the wheel of the brown cargo van sharply to the right, aiming the nose of the vehicle at a concrete culvert in the ditch. Closing my eyes tightly, I gripped the steering wheel.

With my eyes still closed, I felt the jolting of the floor

187

beneath me and heard the scraping of metal. Suddenly, I felt the van fly up into the air. It landed with a giant thud; then everything was silent.

I slowly opened my eyes. My rear end and back throbbed despite the cushioning in the captain's seat. Anxiously, I looked at Thomas. He was in his seat, conscious, with a large cut on his forehead. From our lofty, grassy hillside, which was about 200 feet from the road, I could see the state highway truck and the workers scrambling toward us.

We yelled, "We're okay! Call a tow truck!" Our hands met in a tight clasp as we walked unsteadily down the knoll. It reminded me of our closeness that morning in the restaurant.

The workers approached us quickly, tossing off their hats and screaming, "We're coming—just stay put!"

Thomas and I looked back at the van. Its front tires were flat, steam exited from the radiator in several different places, and the right front panel and headlight were severely dented.

Our ride in the tow truck was joyous. We told Ed, the driver, all about the accident and the chubby highway worker as we sat squeezed in the front seat. He dropped our van off at his shop and took us a mile up the street to a tiny motel with a diner attached to it. The motel room was dark, but I felt peaceful and thankful. We both felt the need to kneel down and pray; it was the first time I'd done this with my husband by my side.

P.S. The road crew was cited for operating without proper distance from a merge lane. Four days later, the van was repaired and the fifth anniversary of our love and life was happily celebrated at the Gateway Arch.

How Far Is That Mountain, Gerome?

by Ray Kozakewicz

NINE TIMES OUT OF 10 my wife and I easily agree on vacations. San Francisco, New York City, Lake Tahoe, Santa Fe, Denver, San Antonio and even Biloxi have been enjoyable and relaxing destinations.

But when Anita suggested we take a seven-day walking trip to the Provence region of France, I was certain it would never go beyond the brochure stage. Exercise and the outdoors seldom excite my wife of 30-plus years, except for a short walk in the snow.

Since the trip would be in late September, I doubted we would see snow, even in the Luberon Mountains.

"Come on, Anita, when's the last time you took a walk in the woods or a walk anywhere?" I asked.

"Well, I'll go alone," she responded. Translation, you better come or else.

One of Anita's friends had been on walking trips. "You see and experience more of the country by spending eight hours a day outdoors," she said. Who were we to disagree?

After detailed conversations with the New York travel agent who represented the French walking tour company, some of my concerns were allayed.

Other Americans our age would be in on the walk, the guide would be English speaking, and we would stay at bed and breakfasts with bathrooms. All of our food would be provided. But the terrain would be moderate to difficult, and we would cover from six to 10 miles a day. "If you were looking for a hiking trip, this would not be the trip to take," the agent emphasized.

Since we were in our early 50s and a little overweight, I wondered if we needed a doctor's okay. My exercise amounted to 10 minutes a day on a stationary bike. Anita's conditioning was of particular concern. Walking along high-priced shopping districts in Santa Fe or along 5th Avenue in New York City was the perfect Anita workout.

Still, Provence seemed like a great place to walk for seven days. Wine and cheese. Bread with every meal. The gorgeous flowers. The land of Cézanne, Van Gogh and Picasso. The sweet smells from the brilliant lavender fields alone would make it memorable.

"The guide will also arrange for a van to pick walkers up after lunch if you don't want to walk the rest of the day," Anita noted.

Our family doctor thought it would be a good vacation trip as long as we trained properly. The next couple of months were spent walking four- to six-mile training sessions, about three days a week. And since we lived in Louisiana at the time, we walked early in the summer mornings or after 7 p.m. when it had cooled down to 85 or so.

By mid-September, we were in great shape. Then, two days before the trip Anita fell while walking on a sidewalk, twisting her ankle. It swelled up and was sore, but she remained game.

We left the U.S. on Friday night and arrived in Marseilles late Saturday afternoon. Anita's suitcase didn't. The airline clerk made arrangements to deliver the lost luggage to our hotel in Avigion, about two hours away.

That night we walked the city's historic district. The following morning we met two of the other couples on our trip and then headed by van to Apt, where the rest of our party would join us and the walk would begin. The 30-minute drive took us past farms and several small villages. This flat countryside would not present any difficulties. Driving up to a small group of shops we saw a smiling, black-haired young man in walking shorts.

He introduced himself quietly. "Bonjour, I am Gerome."

Gerome had several boxes of food with him, including wine and cheese. That would be lunch, I assumed. A picnic in the thick forests of Provence would be great.

We divided up the food among the nine of us. I decided to take some of the heavier stuff and gave loaves of bread to Anita to carry in her backpack.

Gerome examined all of our shoes and noticed Dick was wearing leather shoes. "Do you have walking shoes?" he asked politely.

"No, Gerome. These are all I will need."

The morning was fairly easy as we crossed fields following a small stone wall for several miles. We made short stops as Gerome explained in a mixture of French and broken English the names of the trees and plants. Although a little muddy from rains the previous day, we had no problems. We walked in the back of the group getting to know Dick and Carol.

Fall had come to rural Provence, and the lavender had disappeared. But we could still smell the flowers. Gerome paused to continue explaining the sights.

By late morning we came upon a charming village on the side of a small mountain. Since it was Sunday, the entire village was in church. We rested on benches next to a fountain and took photos. Our group then started a two-hour trek along a more difficult route. It was muddy and steep. Continuing upward, we had to be cautious since the footing was not secure.

At midday we reached several huge rocks that overlooked a massive valley. It was impressive. The morning fog had lifted, and we saw many of the farms we had crossed as well as a tiny village up on a mountainside. "How far is that mountain, Gerome?"

He smiled. "About three hours." I heard that a lot over the next week.

Sitting on the rocks, we divided up the food. I took off my shoes and changed to a dry pair of socks. Gerome took a short nap. The sun felt good. The rest felt good for all of us.

As the afternoon wore on, we climbed higher along narrow dirt and rock paths, sometimes crossing isolated roads. Many of us slipped and lost our balance. The walk turned into a serious hike.

Anita was a trouper but was losing her enthusiasm. Several times, she said she would have to quit. "The whole trip can't be this bad." I told her.

Anita's pace gradually slowed as her ankle worsened and we walked on another dirt road that seemed to head straight up to a mountain. Finally, we saw a series of stone buildings and hoped this would be our destination, a comfortable bed and breakfast.

We were joined by a late arrival, our 10th member, a young woman from New York named Ann. I stopped short when she said she was a travel writer who recently had been to the base camp at Mt. Everest.

Our hosts escorted us to our room. It reminded me of a prison cell. Do they give negative stars?

Anita was upset by the lack of heat and minimal lighting. We were exhausted and wanted a hot shower. The bathroom did have a corner where there was a shower of sorts. At dinner, we learned our room must have been the deluxe model. Ann only had a bed. No night tables, chairs or soap. I offered her some of our soap.

The owners of the French walking tour company joined us for dinner, and we shared some concerns about the day's difficulties. They were apologetic about their brochure translations and explained we would be hiking in much more difficult mountain terrain the following day.

After a breakfast of bread, juice and coffee, we set out about 9 a.m. Anita was smiling, but her sore ankle was making it difficult to put much pressure on it. And it was cold outside.

"I am quitting, I can't do it," Anita said.

"Let's try. Take your time, and I'll help you," I said.

Gerome noticed we were far behind and came to check on Anita.

"This is too hard for me, Gerome. You need to arrange a van for me," Anita told him.

He said the next hour would be difficult, but the rest of the day would be easier.

In the afternoon we spent some time in a delightful town called Cucuron, resting in the square with drinks and snacks.

Our bed and breakfast that night was a cozy and friendly inn with clean and bright rooms with bathtubs and showers. Everyone was happy.

Gerome said he would arrange for a taxi after lunch the

next day to take Anita to the next bed and breakfast. Two others planned to join her.

"The morning will be easy," Gerome promised. He was right. Our group walked along flat, paved roads and strolled into Lourmarin, another small village, about 11 a.m.

After another picnic lunch under a grove of trees just outside town, Anita, Carol and Dick left us for the cab, and the group headed high up into the hills. I was in trouble. The hot sun beat down, and we kept climbing on a narrow path. My feet started sliding, and I could feel blisters forming over my toes. Over the next two hours, we stopped often for water breaks, and everyone helped each other. I kept walking and pushing my sore feet in front of me.

About 3 p.m., we reached the summit of the highest mountain I ever wanted to see. We dropped on the ground and congratulated each other. Off in the distance, I saw another mountain and asked Gerome again, "How far is that mountain?"

"About three hours."

"Is that where we are staying tonight?"

"See that mountain on the other side? That's where we are going."

One problem with hiking up a mountain is that you have to hike down. The downward trek along rocky paths offered little support for my shoes, and my blistered feet kept sliding.

"Gerome, it's too far to that mountain."

"We can rest a little longer."

I walked slowly to our next destination, a great little bed and breakfast. Our whole group was exhausted. Anita bought chocolate candy for everyone, and we devoured it after sinking into chairs on the patio. I decided to rest the next day. Anita smiled. She had thrown her walking shoes into the garbage.

We took a cab to Avigion.

A Chilly Christmas

by Regina Weston

On December 19 I called my baby sister in New York with good news. My two boys and I were packing our clothes and beginning a drive from our home in Washington, N.C., to Brooklyn. "Stay home," she said. "I don't want any company right now." I ignored her.

Instead of decorating a tree at home, I put the suitcases and my boys in the car and began our drive north. When we reached Williamston, N.C., I realized I had forgotten to bring the caps needed for operating my portable dialysis machine. That mistake, plus my sister's negativity, should have been enough to convince me to spend Christmas at home. But I was determined to get to Brooklyn, where I knew the children would have an experience that would remain in their hearts for the rest of their lives. After re-turning home to pick up the missing caps I resumed the journey. It was snowing, but I knew I could make it to New York before the flurries turned into a blizzard.

By the time I reached Virginia, the snow was coming down so hard traffic had slowed to 20 miles an hour. I thought about pulling over and staying in a hotel, but that would be too expensive. The New Jersey turnpike was an adventure. Many of the drivers sped along, talking on their cell phones as if it was a bright, sunny day. My car kept sliding around, and on several occasions it drifted off onto the shoulder. Trucks whizzed by with no apparent concern for the weather, spraying my windshield with blinding clouds of snow. The windshield wipers were barely equal to the challenge.

I should have pulled over and waited for the storm to let up. But I was eager to reach my sister's home and a blessed family Christmas reunion just a few hours away. When we finally reached Flatbush in Brooklyn, the blizzard had virtually shut down traffic.

But this was nothing compared to the reception inside. I decided to try to make the best of the visit, but my sister made it clear that the holiday would have gone better without us.

After Christmas the snow melted. The three of us packed our belongings and left without saying goodbye. I now knew that when someone tells you they don't want company it's better to just stay home. I also learned it's a mistake to try to beat Mother Nature. You can't win.

When I returned to North Carolina, my sister called to apologize for the way she treated us. I forgave her, but next Christmas I think I'll try a different vacation. To someplace warmer.

I Think It Was Something I Ate

by Karin Palmquist

I WAS SITTING IN A DOCTOR'S OFFICE in a small town in northern Sweden right before Christmas. It was mid-afternoon, and the sun was already setting.

A young doctor with wire rim glasses and a narrow neck entered the room and looked at my chart.

"Your birthday is coming up. So is mine. You're two years older than me."

Nice introduction. I felt old. Since when were kids younger than me allowed to be doctors?

"So how are you feeling?"

"I have a terrible stomach cramp, and I have not kept down any food for a month."

"What do you do?"

"I'm a writer. I travel a lot."

"So you think it could have been something you ate?"

I had seen the inside of doctor's offices on five continents. It was the downside of traveling. I always got sick. I came home from one trip to Central Asia a rattling 115 pounds, and that's not attractive when you're 6 feet tall, no matter what the fashion mags tells you.

"How is your stress level at work?"

Come on. Enough with the small talk. It wasn't stress. It was something I ate. It started on my trip to Egypt. Just give me something that will knock me out for a couple of days and then I'll be fine.

"These pills they gave you, in . . . " the doctor looked at the chart, "in America. They're strong enough to knock out a horse. I'd never prescribe those pills to a woman." He wrinkled his forehead for emphasis.

"But they worked," I grumbled.

"I really think we need to get to the bottom of this."

Oh no, he was one of those thorough, enthusiastic ones. Get me a jaded one who has been on his shift since Friday and would be just so happy to write me a prescription and get me out of here.

"I'd like to take a look at your intestines."

"You mean like an X-ray?"

"Not quite. It's a procedure called endoscopy. We enter the large intestine with a tiny camera."

A butt cam? Not a pretty picture.

Could this be the end of my travels?

"You have to try to be a bit more careful," the doctor sighed as he wrote out a prescription for something strong, sure to knock me out for a couple of days. It was better than an endoscopy, which I refused.

I hate being careful. Some of my best travel memories are dinner, not to mention breakfast and lunch.

In fact, one of my earliest travel memories also happens to be a meal. I was 5 years old, and my parents and I were driving down from our home in northern Sweden to Warsaw to visit my Polish aunt and uncle.

We disembarked from the overnight ferry in Gdansk early in the morning, before the banks opened. This was the late '70s and Poland was firmly wedged into the Eastern Bloc. The zloty was not a convertible currency. You could only get zlotys in certain Polish locations. There were no Thomas Cook desks when you stepped off the ferry, no exchange offices open 24 hours.

Instead of waiting around, we started driving toward Warsaw. All we had to eat were candy bars. The road wound down the Polish countryside, past grazing cattle and wheat fields. An old woman was walking along the side of the road, carrying a big basket. My dad pulled over and asked the woman what was in her basket.

Apples.

He tried to buy a few with Swedish money that had no value in Poland.

She peeked into the car and her face lit up at the sight of ball point pens.

After my father handed her the pens she said, "Papyrus, papyrus."

"Paper," my dad said, "she wants paper." My parents started scrambling around purses and bags looking for paper.

"Here," I said holding out my coloring book.

My dad quickly bartered the coloring book for apples.

Other memories from that trip have faded, but I do remember sitting in the back seat of our old Citroën, eating my apple, wondering if the woman was coloring the book. It looked like a regular apple but tasted very different. It was a foreign apple in a foreign land. Plus my mom had cleaned it with a perfumed wet wipe.

As I grew up, the less appetizing the food experience, the more cherished the memory. I'd come home telling friends about sheep eyeballs in Kyrgyzstan and deep-fried dragonflies in Indonesia.

At a reception in Iceland my friend Marianne and I

were served some huge lumps of sour-smelling meat. These were definitely not Swedish meatballs. Before refrigerators and takeout, people had to think of other creative ways to preserve food. One was pickling meat, fish and vegetables, leaving a faint smell of vinegar lingering over the island. Fair enough. We didn't mind the pickling but insisted on full disclosure.

"Ram testicles."

Really? So big? Our eyes couldn't help wandering over to the buffet table to perhaps catch a glance of the rest of the smorgasbord.

"Do you have a brother?" Marianne cooed to the ball on her plate as I tried my best to dissect mine without shooting it across the table.

Once after a visit to a mine near Karakol, Kyrgyzstan, my travel mate and I were invited to stay with a local family in a mountain village. We arrived at their house and found the whole family, plus half the village, seated around a table absolutely piled with food. A huge silver samovar filled with tea towered above the cabbage salads, tiny deep-fried, moon-shaped breads and homemade preserves. Someone had told the village people that we were vegetarians. The rumor was false, but after a certain amount of time in Kyrgyzstan and a certain amount of mystery meat, nearly every visitor becomes a vegetarian.

We sat down on one of the thick mattresses next to the table. There was no electricity, and the only source of light in the room was a kerosene lamp. Prodded by the woman of the house, we grazed on Kyrgystan haute cuisine. No one else touched the food. They were watching us chow down, waiting for us to call for seconds.

After dinner we retired to the front room of the three-room house. Seated on mattresses around a low coffee table our hostess offered us an after-dinner drink made from flour and milk. It was the middle of winter and we were at 12,000 feet. Plastic film covered the windows. Clearly these people were heeding the U.S. Department of Homeland Security advice on how to prepare for terrorists. The drink warmed our stomachs, and we emptied our glasses. The woman happily poured another round. We sat there all night, drinking with the village people. After the guests left, our hostess recycled what was left of the drinks back into the bucket.

I love the way people help you appreciate their culinary culture. Of course, sometimes the joke is at your expense. You politely sample the fried caterpillars and then turn around to watch the locals snub the stuff. They don't like it. They just want to haze you like a fraternity initiate. I learned about this first-hand when, as a punishment for my sins, I became a high school exchange student in a tiny West Virginia town. I came expecting cheeseburgers and ended up sampling squirrel stew. I know the main reason they served it was to laugh at a foreigner. After all, we were there for their amusement. I learned a lot during my year in West Virginia. It was exciting to discover that you could make salad out of jello and marshmallows.

Of course there are ways to play it safe. On my last visit to Kyrgyzstan, the French army brought in bottled Evian from France for wimpy soldiers stationed just outside the Kyrgyz capital. But I can't live that way. I can't give up eating local cuisine. I'll continue eating from street kitchens even if I know that there isn't a single squirrel in the entire neighborhood.

My Evening with George Shearing

by Douglas Johnston

WHENEVER I HEAR ENGLISH JAZZ PIANIST GEORGE SHEARING on
the radio, or see his CDs in a record store or read about
one of his concerts, I mentally wince. That's no knock on
Shearing. At 82, he's still a master jazzman and regarded
as an icon of living jazz history.

The George Shearing Quartet's performance at the
George Weston Recital Hall in Toronto recently brought
back a memory.

In September 1970 I was a Winnipeg teenager in England for the first time. Traveling solo and loving every minute of it, I toured around London for a week, then took a
side trip to rural Kent.

I spent a couple of days in and around Canterbury. One
morning I trekked to the Dover coast and took the ferry
across the English Channel to Calais. The next day I returned to London and booked into a youth hostel near
Marylebone Station.

There I met an American girl from Ohio. She was a couple years older than me, but we hit it off and traipsed around
London. One morning over breakfast she asked me if I'd like to
go with her that evening to hear George Shearing play. Though
I'd heard of Shearing, I was no jazz fan, much preferring the
rock 'n' roll gods of the day. Nonetheless, enamored of her and
open to music of any genre, I agreed to go.

For reasons I no longer recall, we were late leaving the hostel that evening. And, as luck would have it, we just missed our train at Marylebone Station, setting us back another 10 minutes. As a result, we were late to the concert.

The jazz club where Shearing played held, maybe, 300 people. All seating was at small tables for four. The place was packed when we arrived. We wended our way through the sea of tables until we spied two empty seats near the middle of the room.

As we were making our way, Shearing and his quartet came on stage to a round of applause. No one introduced him and the band. They just entered and assumed positions.

We were about 15 feet from our target table when Shearing at keyboard started the intro to a song. Just as we reached our seats, I lost my balance. Trying to regain it, I grabbed one of the two empty chairs. But I caught only a corner of it, and chair and I crashed hard and loud to the wood floor.

Unhurt but embarrassed, I jumped up at the precise moment Shearing stopped playing. Slowly turning to the audience, he said, "Oh, I'm sorry. I thought everyone was seated."

Three hundred pairs of eyes fixed on me. Some were bemused. But most were annoyed by my klutzy entrance. I had destroyed the rhythm of the performance. Mumbling "Excuse me," I righted the chair and sat down. After about 15 seconds, Shearing started in on the piece again. I moved nary a muscle for the rest of the concert.

I'll always remember Shearing's graciousness of that evening, which multiplied my humiliation many times over. All in the club had seen who was late, who was klutzy and who was at fault.

Except, of course, George Shearing—who is blind.

The Midnight Bus

by Rachel Warach

I STEPPED JAUNTILY ONTO THE MIDNIGHT BUS. I had my Discman full of fresh batteries, my sleeping bag ready for warmth or as a place to lean my head and lots of snacks for the 24-hour journey.

Heading from Vientiene, Laos, to Hanoi, Vietnam, I had determined that a "luxury" or "tourist" bus wasn't worth the extra expense and hopped a local. This was the way to meet the people and have an experience that wasn't colored by mass tourism.

Every couple of minutes our bus shuddered to a stop. Off trooped the men to push it back to life. As it started gaining speed, the men would run alongside and jump aboard. Twice someone didn't make it back and his wife, toting bags of rice and bundled up babies, would yell out the window. I imagine it was the Vietnamese equivalent of "catch you on the flip side."

When we reached the border early the next morning, the passengers sprang into gear. Boxes were pulled from underneath the bus and placed in the aisle. The pile grew higher and higher until I realized that if I was going to make it through customs, I'd better climb out before I was boxed in. I wondered why the boxes—seemingly riding so well underneath the bus—were suddenly riding with us. But I couldn't give it much thought, as it was time to grease the palms of the customs agents.

An hour and many dollars later, I reboarded. The boxes were heaped in the aisle, on seats and in people's laps. I picked the way to my seat and balanced two boxes on each knee.

Once everyone found a perching place among the crates, the bus headed off down the road. I spent the next hour pinching my legs to regain feeling. The bus screeched to a halt.

Everyone sprang to life and began lifting boxes off the floor, the seats and me. An assembly line stowed the boxes under the bus. Suddenly everything became clear. Out from under the bus crawled our bleary-eyed border hoppers.

The legals and illegals resettled and prepared for the last leg of the journey. The tourists were getting upset about the fact that our bus was heading to the southern Vietnamese town of Hue rather than Hanoi in the north.

A spokesperson was chosen, who made his way to the front to speak with the driver.

"Well?" I asked when he returned. "What happened?"

He shrugged. "We're going to Hue."

Obviously our Hanoi tickets weren't being honored.

"Tell him we can't . . . we won't go to Hue. We'll tell the police . . . the embassy . . . whatever it takes to get us to Hanoi!"

Our man trudged up to the driver and began an intense conversation. The driver pulled the bus over to the side of the road, turned around to face his passengers, stretched and said, "Vote."

He explained to the locals what was going on and then said, "Hanoi." Our group of six tourists raised our hands.

"Hue," said the driver.

The 60 other Vietnamese passengers on board quickly raised their hands.

The driver smiled, picked his teeth and started the bus. We weren't about to give up. We argued, wheedled, pleaded and appealed to our fellow passengers for help.

Suddenly, the driver turned off the engine and opened the door. He kicked us off at a remote location, miles from the nearest village.

Hours later, I spotted another bus headed north. The group made a human chain across the road, forcing the vehicle to stop. Our spokesman boarded and explained the problem. After paying a second bus fare, we were finally on the road to Hanoi.

Civil disobedience can certainly make a trip worthwhile.

Editor's Note: It's not easy being on the road. Particularly if you want to avoid ending up on the Transportation Security Administration's "No Fly" list.

Committed as we are to safe travel, the editors urge you read the government's fine print before leaving on your next journey. And if you don't have time, then follow the advice of travel writer Ellen Creager, who knows all the rules.

Annie, Get Your Stun Gun at Baggage Claim

By Ellen Creager

DON'T YOU JUST HATE IT when you forget that you packed a loaded handgun in your luggage? All that embarrassing airport security. All the hoopla. It's probably happened to you, just like it did to former Detroit Police Chief Jerry Oliver. The chief apparently stowed an unregistered and loaded .25-caliber handgun in his suitcase.

But Oliver isn't the only absentminded tourist. An assistant Macomb County prosecutor got caught with a 5-inch-long steak knife in his carry-on bag at Detroit Metro Airport. Oops, a little slip, he explained. It's not my knife, he said. I mean, it's . . .. He was detained for 20 minutes.

So here's some advice for taking your favorite lethal weapons onto a plane: Your unloaded rifles, switchblades, ice picks, sabers and so forth must go into checked luggage. Nunchakus may seem like a carry-on item, but they're not.

The Transportation Security Administration also reminds you that BB guns, cattle prods, crowbars, mace, billy clubs and brass knuckles have to be checked. Don't you feel safer just knowing that your mild-mannered seat-mate's rifle and meat cleaver are tucked away in the belly of the plane?

My brother-in-law's father once carried a decorative axe all the way home from Germany, and nobody cared. But that was before Sept. 11. Somehow, I thought that these days all sharp objects or anything that could go boom would be kept off our flights.

But the TSA can be surprisingly permissive. Sure, hand grenades, dynamite, gasoline, spray paint, tear gas and fireworks are banned, but bullets can be carry-on items on some airlines as long as they're "securely packed in fiber, wood or metal boxes."

And as long as you check them, you can also take your favorite unloaded firearms, throwing stars, stun guns, compressed air guns, pellet guns, starter pistols, etc. Ditto for your hatchets, scissors, box cutters, hammers and other tools. Also welcome in checked luggage are swords, ice picks and meat cleavers. As long as they're checked, bows and arrows are fine; so are baseball bats, golf clubs, pool cues, hockey sticks, ski poles and spear guns.

No wonder passengers are having trouble meeting the airlines' new 50-pound baggage limit. Do you have any idea how much a meat cleaver weighs? Meanwhile, experts have concluded that eyelash curlers are not lethal weapons, meaning they are welcome in carry-on bags. Also allowed as carry-ons are knitting and crochet needles (ouch), corkscrews, cigar cutters, cuticle cutters, eyeglass repair tools, plastic or round-bladed knives. Four books of safety matches are fine, and so are your nail clippers, nail files, aerosol hair spray or deodorant, safety razors and blunt-tip scissors.

Your kids' Transformers (robot toys) are OK. So are tweezers, umbrellas, walking canes, braille note takers, diabetes-related equipment, nitroglycerine pills, prosthetic devices, camcorders, laptop computers, mobile phones, pagers and PDAs.

But no loaded guns. No carry-on steak knives. Keep your nunchakus. Just make sure to check 'em.

About the Authors

Pamela Alma Bass

Pamela Alma Bass is a graduate of the MFA in creative writing program at the University of San Francisco. Her writing can also be found in *Hot Flashes: Sexy Little Stories and Poems*. She is currently at work on a novel. She and Stephen (the man who dragged her to "Earthdance") were married in October, 2003, which proves that sometimes there are rewards for suffering.

Lisa Alpine

Lisa Alpine is an addicted traveler who always turns her passion into a career. She has been a professional writer for 21 years and is the travel columnist for the *Pacific Sun* in Marin County, California. Her articles and short stories have appeared in numerous periodicals and anthologies. When not acting as a book midwife and writing coach, she works as a freelance feature writer and teaches writing (www.lisaalpine.com) at The Writing Salon in San Francisco and Book Passage in Corte Madera and at her home studio. She's also a proud member of the infamous writing group, The Wild Writing Women.

Linda Ballou

Blessed with a double dose of genetic wanderlust, Linda Ballou loves to explore. Her pioneering parents took her to Alaska when she was 13, where she became firmly grounded in nature. From there she journeyed to California and obtained a degree in English literature. Today, she is a freelance writer based in Los Angeles, specializing in soft outdoor adventures.

Her mission is to experience as many beautiful places on our planet as she can, before they are no more. Presently, she is working on "Great Outdoor Days in L.A.," short pieces that take the reader on daytrips into the Santa Monica Mountains. Her byline has appeared in numerous national magazines as well as the *Los Angeles Times*.

Marilou Brewer

The author has most unpleasantly "sicked" herself out of numerous places as soon as the going gets rough. She is familiar with the medical system in at least a dozen different countries. Simple solution, she stayed home after having a son in Australia and became a naturopath. Danger lurks, as she will soon be living in Fiji.

Fern Burch

Although many children reluctantly write about their summer vacations under a teacher's stern glare, few continue this crazed behavior into adulthood. Fern Burch always wanted to be a writer, even in the first grade, when she would come home from school and write endless books, all on the subject of little girls and horses. She was finally liberated to live her own true-life adventure as she completed a 3,000-mile drive from the East Coast and landed in Berkeley, California.

She met the love of her life, the King of Hearts, at a Halloween party. They eloped in a Medici Palace in Florence, Italy, and are still traveling companions today.

Diane Carlson

One of Diane Carlson's favorite things in the world is traveling with her partner, Keith, and daughter, Zoë. They have ventured to many places including China, Thailand and Guatemala. As much as Diane loves to travel, it is still difficult to leave behind the family's three dogs, Bandit, Chani and Aiki. When not traveling, Diane practices Okazaki Restorative Massage and researches, writes and illustrates children's books on subjects including traveling, peace and diversity. She trains in DanZanRyu Jujitsu, regardless of geographical location. Diane and her family live in Davis, California.

Seymour Collins

Seymour Collins is a retired mechanical engineer who has written and self-published his autobiography and four other books. He writes plays, poetry, fiction and non-fiction, and his essays cover a wide range of subjects, some humorous, some serious. Formerly a long-time resident of Oakland, California, he now resides in Medford, Oregon, with his wife, Annie, and their used Anatolian shepherd, Yum Yum. His book, *Travels With the Gods,* includes an essay entitled "That's Flatbush—I Once Lived There." It is a memoir inspired by a long-delayed return visit to the Brooklyn of his childhood.

Ellen Creager

Ellen Creager is the travel writer at the *Detroit Free Press.*

Hannah Ruth Davis

Hannah Ruth Davis is from a family of eight. Growing up with so many siblings and two eccentric parents allowed for many of the "out of the ordinary" experiences that continue to this day. She is now a sophomore studying acting at the University of North Carolina at Greensboro. Although she was only nine at the time of writing her story, she comments that "this situation as well as many others have stuck with me throughout my entire life and have created a more colorful spectrum that I have been able to use to help me as an actor."

Laura Deutsch
Laura Deutsch is a writer, writing coach, editor and teacher based in Mill Valley, California. Her personal essays, news-features, travel and humor pieces have appeared in the *New York Times, More* magazine, *Mademoiselle,* the *ABA Journal,* the *Dallas Morning News* and a travel book published by Simon & Schuster, among other publications. Her broadcasting experience includes work with KQED, the San Francisco Bay Area's public television station, and her commentary has aired on "Perspectives," a regular feature on KQED-FM public radio.

Bob Drews
Bob Drews is a book editor and author of two novels. He and his family live in San Jose, California.

Tom DuBois
Tom DuBois is an inventor (of the San Francisco Penny Machine, a gizmo that turns pennies into souvenirs) and businessman who lives in Ashland, Oregon, with his wife, Monika, and daughters Maelia, 14, and Anja, 12. His family's best times are spent exploring our western National Parks.

Nola M. Dunbar

Nola M. Dunbar writes and lives in her rural eastern North Carolina home, where her husband of 35 years and their 11-year-old standard schnauzer are her companions. She has two grown sons and three grandchildren, and she manages the family farm.

During her early years, she lived and traveled as a military housewife within the Southwest and Australia. More recently, she worked for more than 16 years in management positions at a direct-mail company. As the plant closed, Nola returned to college at age 51. There, she developed a passion for writing and photography, strangely following in her younger son's footsteps. She enjoys writing short stories to document family history and her travels. Her first short story was published in 2003.

Russ Faure-Brac

Faure-Brac has been going on adventure trips for 30 years, including mountain climbing, river rafting, sea kayaking, canyoneering and river boarding. He has two grown sons with whom he has shared many epics. Since retiring from a career in environmental planning, he has lived on a horse ranch in west Marin County, California. His idea of adventure travel now is to crew for his wife's multi-day endurance rides where she rides the horse across the desert and he drives the truck in the comfort of air conditioning and stereo music.

Charles Finley

In an earlier life, Charlie Finley was a forester, and for 25 years the executive director of the Virginia Forestry Association. Having retired several times unsuccessfully, he bills himself now as an "urban migrant worker" in Richmond, Virginia, and runs a business named Verbatim Editing.

As an editor and part-time writer he coaches those who wish to self-publish and market their works. Other canoe adventures include 150 miles on the Allagash Whitewater Wilderness in northern Maine over an 11-day period, and 130 miles on the Buffalo River in Arkansas.

Polly Greist

Polly Greist has been an instructor of composition and literature at numerous colleges in California. Upon moving to southern Oregon, she and husband Bill Cross ran a small whitewater instruction school, Running Wild. She and Bill live with their three children in Ashland, along with her saxophone and Conga and Taiko drums. Rafting the great rivers of the West, Rockies and Southwest is her passion, and for those trips she relies upon her toy accordion.

Jean B. Hauser

Born in Harrow, England, in 1942, Jean Hauser worked as a horse trainer until 1967, when she came to the United States to train horses for foxhunting. She now works as an independent trainer and is married with one son and two grandchildren. She lives in Virginia with her husband, James, and a Treeing Feist squirrel dog. Her hobbies are reading and gardening.

Candace Hisert

When she is not giving tours or lectures for the Fine Arts Museums in San Francisco, you can find Candace Hisert performing marriages both in her capacity as a minister of the Universal Life Church and as a county deputy. She also attempts to bring some art history to children in the Oakland, California public schools. With her husband she has worked in Pompeii, measuring houses, and in Petra, where she discovered the capital of a column (it was too big not to be discovered).

Alison James

Alison James is an author, actress and financier. Her first book, *I Used to Miss Him . . . But My Aim is Improving (Not Your Ordinary Breakup Survival Guide)*, is a sassy, edgy guide offering practical advice with a "rip his head off" twist. She also works as a financial manager for A&E and the History Channel in Manhattan.

Alison grew up in Upstate, New York, received a B.A. from Princeton University's Woodrow Wilson School and then won a scholarship to study at the London School of Economics where she earned a master's of science in public policy. She resides in New York City with her phobic fiancé and her cat.

Douglas J. Johnston

Douglas J. Johnston is a Winnipeg lawyer and writer.

Joe Kempkes

Joe Kempkes' feature article telling of his experiences counting homeless people in soup kitchens and under highway overpasses at 3 a.m. during the 2000 U.S. Census won first prize among California journalism students. He lives in Oakland and writes film reviews for Laney Tower and RottenTomatoes.com. Read his interview of filmmaker Michael Moore at www.interlog.com/~kempkes/joe/.

Kim Klescewski

Kim Klescewski has edited a number of books for RDR Books, including *I Should Have Just Stayed Home*, *I Should Have Gone Home*, *The Wannabe Guide to Music* and *Foiled: Hitler's Jewish Olympian*.

Bryan Vincent Knapp

Novelist and editor Bryan Vincent Knapp was a Cold War baby. Born at NATO headquarters, he spent his early life boldly facing the Iron Curtain. Knapp says Big Macs on the Hauptstrasse in Heidelberg are what ultimately did in the Soviet Union (you know, a battle of systems). He has traveled extensively, studied faithfully under the Guru of Travel Trouble and set more than two million words to the page.

Ray Kozakewicz

Ray Kozakewicz is a former newspaper reporter and sports writer and currently a public relations manager with a large media and broadcast company in Richmond, Virginia, who edits a non-profit bi-monthly newspaper. Since his walking trip to France, he has only taken vacations on flat land or on cruises.

Jim Krois

Jim Krois is a gray-haired grandpa who grew up in the midst of San Francisco's hippie revolution and, after spending a year and a half traveling around the world in the late '70s, moved to Oregon. In 2003 he received a bachelor's degree in photojournalism from Southern Oregon University with a minor in applied multimedia. He is a member of the Oregon Poetry Association and has published four chapbooks of poetry and written a book of creative non-fiction. The Rogue Community College's Wiseman Gallery annex has displayed Jim's pictures of Costa Rican children, his poetry and photo/art work have appeared in previous editions of the *Rogue's Gallery Literary Magazine* and *Manzanita Quarterly,* and he has won awards for his photos at local art shows.

Jim lives with his wife, Catherine, in Williams, Oregon, and works as a staff photographer for the Grants Pass Daily Courier.

Karen Kutney
Karen Kutney is a small-animal veterinarian who lives and works in Vancouver, British Columbia. She shares her home with her husband, Joe, rottweiler Khyanna and black cat, Lorenzo, all of whom are very supportive of her writing. This is her first published work.

Shirley Lawyer
Shirley Lawyer works in human resources recruiting in Medford, Oregon. She also volunteers as a reading tutor in the Start Making A Reader Today (SMART) program at Wilson Elementary School. In addition to travel tales, she enjoys writing employment advertising and bad poetry. Recent adventures include a run-in with a dead whale on the Oregon coast, a stand-off with a pack of wild dogs on the Rough and Ready Creek trail and a near drowning in the Rogue River. Rogue River rafters and sports fishers please note: A reward is being offered for the return of a green daypack containing Shirley's keys and wallet.

Sunny Lucia

Lucia is a veteran adventurer who began independently exploring at 40 years of age after an executive career and raising two children. She took her backpack and soloed through China for a month. She found towns not on maps, rode on every mode of transport, was spat on and invited into homes. Sunny has traveled with her husband on freighters, rafted wild rivers and hired donkey carts in 38 countries. She has written a book on travel for couples.

Tina Martin

Martin's travel adventures began when she was 8 years old and "accidentally" flew alone to New York City to join her father at a psychology convention. That experience taught her the importance of making the right mistakes and welcoming unexpected detours from previously made plans.

She applied to the Peace Corps, specifying any French- or Spanish-speaking country and was sent to Tonga, where they speak a Polynesian language in no way related to French or Spanish. Using her Peace Corps readjustment allowance, she traveled to Spain, where she taught English in Madrid for a year and received free French lessons, leading her to Algeria, where she taught at a girls' lycee for two years, which inspired the story "An Algerian Wedding," excerpted in *I Should Have Just Stayed Home*.

Martin is the mother of a 25-year-old son and an instructor at City College of San Francisco, where her ESL students make it possible to travel around the world just by coming to class.

John D. McCafferty

John D. McCafferty is a former English professor at Santa

Barbara City College and copy editor at the Los Angeles Times. He lives in Santa Barbara with his wife, writer Sharon Dirlam. In addition to many short stories and newspaper features, John has published two books: Dick McNabb, Private Dick, a mystery; and Aliso School—For the Mexican Children, the story of school segregation in a California town.

Brenda McGee
Brenda McGee is married and resides in Bath, North Carolina. A native Ohioan, she is a retired science teacher interested in drawing, quilting and collecting Italian pottery. This is her first short story.

Richard Menzies
Richard Menzies lives in Salt Lake City and has written numerous magazine articles about the West. He is co-author of the *Berlitz Travelers Guide to the American Southwest* and also contributed a chapter to *Australia: True Stories of Life Down Under, a Travelers' Tales Guide.* His long-awaited first book, *Passing Through,* was due to be published by Stevens Press in October 2004.

Li Miao
Li Miao writes about cultural and environmental issues from the San Francisco Bay Area. Her work has been appeared in the *San Francisco Chronicle, Sierra Club Planet, Taiwan News* and on KQED public radio. Miao's travels have ranged from the wet and woolly Scottish highlands to the arid sand dunes of the Mojave Desert. An avid hiker, she spent two months backpacking 600 miles of the Appalachian Trail. Camping in primitive shelters, she dealt with bears, mosquitoes and mice, but no plumbing problems.

Elizabeth Mullet
Born in Montana, raised in North Carolina, and with friends and relatives spread in most of the U.S. and various foreign countries, Elizabeth Mullet loves to travel. A nurse, she also does editing, teaches school and revises curriculum for a Christian publishing company. Sometimes, even with careful planning, she still gets into scrapes. But once the situation is past, it makes for an interesting memory.

Ethel F. Mussen
Ethel F. Mussen, a retired speech pathologist and audiologist, was born in Los Angeles in the '20s and grew up with the automobile. A Berkeley resident since 1955 when her late husband joined the faculty of psychology at the University of California, she has driven byways and highways in North America, Europe and Middle East, balking only at New Zealand. She is now engaged in telling stories of her glorious past.

Karin Palmquist
So far, Swedish native Karin Palmquist's career choices have been nothing but elaborate excuses to get the next travel fix. After college (which she divided up between two continents), she worked as a runway model for the wonderful opportunities it offered to see a bit more of the world. At 23, she started working in advertising but quickly realized it wasn't letting her travel enough. A freelance writer for newspapers such as The Washington Times and Washington Post, she now roams the globe about six months a year. The rest of the year she spends in her adopted home of Washington, DC.

Dean Pappas

Dean Pappas is a marketing and promotions professional in Chicago. Writing advertising copy and building marketing campaigns provides him with creative outlets; however, he strives to continue to write short stories, science fiction and screenplays. While his contribution to this book seems to be the material that movies are made of, it is unfortunately true, although the names have been changed to protect the guilty. Dean still frequents Las Vegas and continues to wait for another jackpot. He also has the overwhelming compulsion to be the one to tip the driver whenever he's in a limousine.

Susan Parker

Susan Parker's memoir, *Tumbling After, Pedaling Like Crazy when Life Goes Downhill,* has been optioned for television by HBO. She is fond of small gourds and big margaritas.

Judy Paulsen

Judy Paulsen enjoys living in the beautiful town of Ashland, Oregon, and still enjoys traveling. She was married to husband Wayne for 45 years; they met at Southern Oregon University, and both graduated with BS degrees in Eduation and later received their Masters' Degrees. After 28 years, Judy retired from Walker and Helman Elementary Schools but continues to tutor in her home.

Nadine Michele Payn

Nadine Michele Payn is a clinical psychologist with a practice in Albany/Berkeley, California. She hosted a popular psychology call-in show on KGO radio in the early '80s and was a contributing editor to the *Berkeley Insider* magazine in the mid-'90s. Nadine began traveling at the age of 15 and loves to write about her many adventures and misadventures around the globe.

Carla Perry
Carla Perry is the author of two books of poetry and illustrations: *No Questions Asked, No Answers Given* and *Laughing Like Dogs*. In December 2003, she was awarded the Oregon Governor's Art Award as well as an Oregon Literary Fellowship in Fiction. She is currently working on a novel.

Kristi Porter
Kristi Porter lives in North Muskegon, Michigan, with husband Dennis, son Andy and twin cats, Niki and Noah. A preschool teacher, she won the Governor's Award for her work with young children and is dedicated to promoting reading in the early childhood setting. Her story won the statewide trouble travel contest cosponsored by the *Detroit Free Press*.

Roger Rapoport
Roger Rapoort, the publisher of RDR Books, is co-editor of the *I Should Have Stayed Home* series.

Ellen Rubenson
Ellen Rubenson lives in Ashland, Oregon. A viola player, she is employed as a medical social worker but aspires to be a travel writer. Her publications include *When Aging Parents Can't Live Alone* and an article, "Journey to the Kuna Yala Archipelago of Panama."

Rachel Seed

Rachel Seed lives and works as a writer and editor in Chicago, though she has called many places home. Born in London, she contracted the travel bug at an early age and considers her dual citizenship to be the perfect antidote.

Don Sweet

Don Sweet, who launched his writing career in the insurance industry, lives in Medford, Oregon with his wife Marilyn.

Lisa Thompson

Lisa Thompson writes about two places: California and Mexico. She lives on Tomales Bay in Inverness, where she swims with her dog, watches the changing light on the east shore and writes www.field-notes.net: Musings about Place, Poetry and Wonder. She has recently completed a children's book, *Feliz Navidad Tortuga*.

Tom Turman

Tom Turman lives in Berkeley, California, and has been an architect and teacher in the Bay Area for 30 years. His story is excerpted from his book *WAWA—West Africa Wins Again*.

Rachel Warach

Rachel Warach spent a year traveling through New Zealand, Australia, Southeast Asia and Southern Africa and concluded that the world is a wonderful and wacky place. She's lived in El Paso, Austin, Portland and Boston and currently makes her home in Chicago. Rachel tells a mean knock-knock joke.

Charles West
Charles West lives in Mendocino, California with his wife Trish. When he chanced to return to Denver aboard Amtrak a few years ago, he remained on the train during the one-hour stopover.

Regina Weston
Regina Weston is a 32-year-old homemaker in Washington, North Carolina. The mother of two boys, she graduated from the College of New Rochelle with a degree in psychology. Her passion, though, is writing. Regina has written several published short stories and poems.

Eugene Wildman
Eugene Wildman has taught at IIT, Northwestern University and the University of Illinois at Chicago, where he is the director of the creative writing program. He is a former editor of the *Chicago Review* and a winner of four Illinois Arts Council awards for fiction. Most of his early work was experimental. He was editor of the *Chicago Review Anthology of Concretism,* the first collection of visual poetry to appear in this country. That was followed by *Experiments in Prose,* an assemblage of nonlinear and mixed media texts. He is also the author of two experimental novels, *Montezuma's Ball* and *Nuclear Love.* His short story collection, *The World of Glass,* was recently released by the University of Notre Dame Press. He is currently at work on a novel and a second collection of short stories.

Don't Forget to Write

RDR Books, the world leader in travel humor, welcomes funny stories about travel disasters. The stories should be 500 to 1,500 words and must be true. They can be emailed to trouble@rdrbooks.com or mailed to RDR Books at 2415 Woolsey, Berkeley, CA 94705. Here are tips from our editors.

1. Keep the "I" under control. Write about the people you meet, others who have shared the unhappy experience. Instead of monologue, consider dialogue.
2. Direct quotes are a good idea. Laugh at yourself. You may have been part of the problem.
3. Show your story to an experienced editor before you submit it. Follow their suggestions. They know what they are doing.
4. Shorten the story to see if you like it better.
5. The royal "we" is the most repeated word in funny travel stories. Try to use other pronoun references.
6. It's a good idea to let the story tell itself. You don't have to explain everything.
7. Read books in our series, available at libraries and bookstores.
8. For more information, consult the "submissions" section at www.rdrbooks.com.

RDR Books thanks you for your submission and will contact you in the event that your story is selected. Please be patient. It may be a number of months until you hear back from us. If you want your story returned, please enclose a self-addressed stamped envelope. RDR Books cannot be responsible for your manuscript. Please do not send us your original. Even the post office makes mistakes. The editors share your pain and look forward to hearing from you. Bon Voyage.

Coming Soon from RDR Books

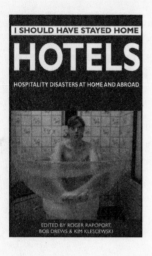

From Madagascar to Mongolia, from the penthouse to the broom closets, you'll read about the lodging industry's secrets and snafus in *I Should Have Stayed Home: HOTELS*, the hilarious book that rolls up the welcome mat. Then there's *I Should Have Stayed Home: FOOD*, in whose pages armchair gourmets are introduced to such cuisine as pan-fried piranha and grilled anteater on the banks of the Amazon, not to mention champagne and caviar on the Trans-Siberian Express.

I Should Have Stayed Home: HOTELS, ISBN 1-57143-120-9, $13.95
I Should Have Stayed Home: FOOD, ISBN 1-57143-121-7, $13.95

And don't miss these *Gone Home* titles, now available from your local bookstore or RDR Books:

I Should Have Stayed Home, ISBN 1-57143-014-8, $17.95
I've Been Gone Far Too Long, ISBN 1-57143-054-7, $17.95
I Really Should Have Stayed Home, ISBN 1-57143-081-4, $17.95
I Should Have Just Stayed Home, ISBN 1-57143--096-2, $17.95